Nineteenth Century Wooden Boxes

Arene Wiemers Burgess

4880 Lower Valley Road, Atglen, PA 19310 USA

Dedication

To my husband, Chuck, who, after thirty-seven years,
has yet to say, "Why did you buy That?"

Acknowledgments

I want to express my gratitude to all who helped in any way with this book. Thanks especially to the following who allowed me to photograph items in their collections: Dianne Burton, Diane Dudley and the dealers at Yesterday's Market, Jim Hunsley, Darlene Lesicko, Rosemary Spoon, and several others who wish to remain anonymous. More important was their willingness to share their knowledge, and for that I thank them all sincerely. Francis Bacon, the sixteenth century English philosopher, said it all with three words, "Knowledge is power."

Copyright © 1997 by Arene Wiemers Burgess
Library of Congress Catalog Card Number: 97-67261

ISBN: 0-7643-0319-8
Printed in China
1 2 3 4

Designed by Bonnie M. Hensley

Published by Schiffer Publishing Ltd.
4880 Lower Valley Road
Atglen, PA 19310
Phone: (610) 593-1777; Fax: (610) 593-2002
E-mail: schifferbk@aol.com
Please write for a free catalog.
This book may be purchased from the publisher.
Please include $3.95 for shipping.
Try your bookstore first.

We are interested in hearing from authors
with book ideas on related subjects.

Contents

This is my box, This is my box, I never travel without my box.

         —from Amahl and the Night Visitors

Introduction

When Adam and Eve left The Garden, what did they use to carry their "stuff?" From the very beginning, men (and women) have had to devise ways to store and transport their belongings. Boxes or coffers are mentioned in ancient writings.

The American Heritage Dictionary of the English Language defines box as "a rectangular container, typically having a lid or cover." This book will attempt to cover only wooden boxes made from about 1790 to 1890. Until the mid-twentieth century, every home utilized wooden boxes: crates from the grocery, cigar boxes, sewing boxes, trunks, etc. Most storage furniture is essentially a box — a chest of drawers is a set of boxes arranged in a frame. Some boxes were considered special from the time they were created, but most were utilitarian — made for use rather than display. Even special boxes such as tea caddies or bride's chests had a practical use. Some types of boxes have been omitted from this book. Advertising boxes, seed boxes, cigar boxes, etc., have not been covered as these are special categories more than adequately covered by other writers.

The nineteenth century was the golden age of the decorated box. Creativity and ingenuity were valued and rewarded by American society. More people were becoming part of the middle class — a large group of Americans that had some discretionary income after their basic needs were met. Mama didn't need to keep her sewing equipment in a sack; the local craftsman could make a nice box (with a lock) out of cherry or walnut. A young woman thinking of marriage needed a box to keep her quilts and linens clean and safe. A large trunk or box with her name on the front was an expected engagement gift. Fads or changes in society required new storage facilities. Tea had to be kept in a closed, dry container. Sugar, too, had to be kept dry and under lock and key. As more people became literate, correspondence and other paper ephemera increased. Lap desks (writing boxes) were something of a status symbol — visible proof of literacy and business affairs. Candles had to be kept safe from rodents.

Needs and wants changed. With the advent of kerosene lamps, candle boxes were no longer needed. The invention of the sewing machine changed storage needs for the needle woman. Many of the old boxes seem to be unique — early craftsmen were not interested in turning out dozens of identical objects. Also, few objects were made on "spec." If someone needed a lap desk or tea caddy, he ordered one. Of course, this changed as nineteenth-century America emerged from a rural society into a machine-driven age.

Some early boxes are marvels of ingenuity. Secret drawers and compartments were more common than rare. The tantalus lived up to its name. Even tills in blanket chests had secret compartments. The inlay or paint work on some box lids held secret messages known only to the maker and the recipient. Elaborate early sewing boxes often had a secret compartment to hold "mad" money or any small things of sentimental or monetary value. The boxes pictured and described range from the simplest to the most ornate. All had a place and a use in nineteenth-century America.

There were several ways in which the material in this book could have been categorized: first, by time frame, which would be difficult since it is impossible to accurately date most boxes unless they were dated by their owner or maker; second, by style, from the simplest to the most ornate; or third, in alphabetical order using commonly accepted names such as blanket box or tea caddy. I chose the third method, though I had qualms about some of the categories. Should original terms or modern ones be used? For instance, the "Bible Box" term was probably not used by the original owner, nor was the term "apple box."

Each chapter begins with a short description of the boxes being categorized. When applicable there is mention of reproductions, signs of age, old methods of construction, etc. The photo captions include sizes, wood, finish, construction details, hardware, and approximate date of construction. Pricing proved difficult — most of the boxes pictured are "one of a kind." Two boxes may appear to be very similar, but the prices are different. The higher-priced one probably has its original finish and hardware. Also some woods are more sought after than others. For example, in the Midwest, cherry or walnut is preferred over pine unless the pine has its original paint. There is a rather strange contradiction between "formal" boxes and "country" pieces. To be salable, a formal piece such as a tea caddy must appear "perfect." Damaged veneer must be repaired. The box should look as if it has never been used. A country piece, on the other hand, should not be stripped, refinished, or otherwise "messed with." Original condition is everything.

This book is meant to be a general overview of boxes available at shows, shops, and malls. For more information on a particular category of boxes, one should consult specialists and books and articles in periodicals such as "Maine Antique Digest," "The Magazine Antiques," and other publications devoted to antiques.

All Carriers, Great and Small

Alms Boxes

The alms box was once part of the furnishings of urban churches and cathedrals. A locked, generally wall-hanging box was kept near the entrance. Parishioners and visitors were expected to contribute coins for the needy of the parish. The boxes are still in place in some older churches but more for symbolism than substance. The boxes are about 12 or 15 inches long, have a slanted lid with a slot, and are simply constructed with little or no ornamentation except for iron hinges and bands.

Alms or collecting box? This odd little box was obviously used for collecting and storing coins. It is not a child's bank. There appears to be no way to remove the coins without dismantling the box. The brass plate is held in place with tiny brass brads. The wood is pine with flame birch veneer. The use of veneer is one indication that this box was more than just a toy or a shop keeper's box. It probably was made for a religious or charitable group. An English coin was found in the box, 5" x 8" x 5", c. 1810, $40 as is.

Apothecary Chests

The apothecary was the predecessor of the druggist or pharmacist. Eighteenth- and nineteenth-century housewives were also versed in the art of healing. Most had herb gardens or gathered herbs from the wild to treat their families and servants. Tinctures were made by brewing and/or adding alcohol to herb leaves or roots.

Apothecary boxes used by doctors, midwives, apothecaries, etc., are generally more elaborate and finely made then the simple boxes pictured in this chapter. Most are in museums or private collections and seldom come on the market. Many herb chests made for home use resemble spice boxes. However, the herb or apothecary chests are larger than spice chests and often have 12 or more drawers. Some are wider than they are long and are mistaken for boxes used by cabinet makers or carpenters to store small items such as nails or screws.

Nine-drawer apothecary chest, maple with old, but not original, red paint, rabbeted drawers, paneled sides. Probably dating from the mid-nineteenth century, the knobs and paint were added around 1900. This dark red, unstable (shellac-based) paint is often found on toys and other objects dating from the turn of the century. (See Trinket Boxes for another example of this dark red paint applied to an older box), 10" x 15-1/2" x 17-1/2", $300.

Apothecary chest, pine, nailed, drawers made from cigar boxes, original salmon paint, original knobs, $425. *Courtesy collection of Darlene Lesicko/made by owner's grandfather.*

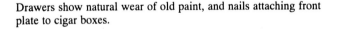

Drawers show natural wear of old paint, and nails attaching front plate to cigar boxes.

Eight-drawer apothecary chest "as found," rabbeted case and drawers, softwood probably pine, 28" x 10" x 9", c. 1880. *Private collection.*

Same chest after cleaning and minor restoration, $245.

Apothecary chest, pine, with original dark brown paint, beaded drawers, paneled sides, unusual top molding, and square nails, 18" x 21" x 7-1/2", c. 1860, $500. *Courtesy collection of Darlene Lesicko.*

Unusual, if not unique, this pine apothecary chest has its original paint and knobs. Half-round shelves may be for mixing or chopping herbs, 16" x 18" x 6-1/2", c. l870, $400. *Courtesy collection of Darlene Lesicko.*

Shelves are mortised into case; traces of first coat of green paint are still visible.

Apple Boxes

Apple box is probably a twentieth-century term. It refers to a square or rectangular lidless box with slanted sides. The wood is generally pine with a natural finish. Originally they might have been used for serving bread or biscuits. Nearly all are nailed rather than dovetailed. They have been reproduced for years. One should look for signs of age and use. Nails are an important clue. Old nails have irregular heads and will show dark brown (not bright orange) rust. Old boxes often have stains that cannot be removed. Apple boxes on pedestals are known but rare. The pedestal types seen at malls and flea markets are not old. They were a popular item in the 1950s and were offered for sale in women's magazines. Most apple boxes are about 12 inches square and 4 inches tall. Some collectors believe these boxes were actually spittoons. They were filled with sand or sawdust to facilitate cleaning.

The inside of this box is dented and stained from use and age.

Square, slant-side apple box in old finish, penciled on bottom, "H. Muller '38." Scooped out (curved) sides are an unusual refinement for an apple box or a spittoon, c. 1880, $200.

Ballot Boxes

Plain rectangular boxes were once used at every polling place to collect and store ballots. The name of the precinct or township was painted or stamped on the side. There was generally a slot in the top for depositing the ballot and a strong lock on the lid. (For another type of ballot box, see Black Ball Boxes.) Many historical societies have one or more ballot boxes in their collections as a reminder to visitors of the way the voting process was once conducted. Between elections the boxes were kept by the precinct chairman, probably in his home. When new methods of voting were introduced, the boxes were discarded. Today, these old boxes are apt to turn up almost anywhere, often unrecognized for what they once were.

The age is difficult to determine for this ballot box, though the square nails indicate pre-1875. Pine, nailed construction, brass lock, sliding top, 8-1/2" x 15" x 8", $80.

Band Boxes

"Band Box" has several connotations. Originally a band box was a round or oval loose-lidded box used primarily by women to hold hats and other articles of clothing. The boxes were often painted with a decorative scene or covered with wallpaper. They were made of light, thin wood or cardboard. Late in the nineteenth century, small round boxes, sometimes made of wood but more often of celluloid, were made to hold men's detachable shirt collars. Some reference books refer to these late boxes as band boxes, though collar boxes would be a more accurate term. The early boxes had no hinges or locks. Finding boxes in good condition is difficult as these band boxes were the "suitcases" of their day. They were subjected to rough handling on wagons and coaches. Rain or snow could ruin the decoration. They were somewhat of a status symbol among young women who worked in the textile factories of New England and it was not unusual for one person to own four or five of these colorful boxes.

All of these "stacked" boxes of various colors from various makers, have their original finish from the nineteenth century, $130 each and up. *Courtesy collection Darlene Lesicko.*

Bentwood Boxes

As the name implies, bentwood boxes were made by bending or shaping a thin, pliable board around a round or oval base. The overlapping ends were riveted together with metal fasteners. The same procedure was used to fashion the lids, which generally were not hinged. These boxes were made and used throughout the nineteenth century and beyond. Some mistakenly refer to all these boxes as Shaker. The Shakers did make these boxes in many sizes, but calling all bentwood boxes Shaker is like calling all china Limoges. The Shaker-made boxes have a unique riveting technique which is familiar to Shaker collectors and devotees. The smallest bentwood boxes (probably used for storing things like pins or seeds) are less than two inches across. The largest ones are bigger than a modern five-gallon pail. Occasionally one can be found with a shaped, wooden handle. Later examples often have a wire bail (handle). A recent fad is collecting and stacking graduated-size boxes in the living or family room, a practice which surely would have puzzled and amused the original owners. Production of these boxes has never stopped. For many years the small, eight-inch size was used commercially as a container for fresh fruits such as blueberries and strawberries. Today new ones can be found in craft stores.

This oval bentwood cheese box is made of pine and fastened with cane webbing and small brads. It originated in Minnesota in the late nineteenth century, 4" x 8" x 4". *Courtesy Dianne L. Burton.*

Oval bentwood boxes, with riveted fingers. The small box has original yellow paint finish, c. 1880; small box on left, $250; larger box, $150. *Courtesy collection of Darlene Lesicko.*

Bible Boxes

This is a commonly accepted and generally used term for a rectangular, hinged, lidded eighteenth century box fitted with a lock and key. Most look like small blanket chests. This term would have been very apropos in the seventeenth and eighteenth centuries when most families owned only one book — the Bible. Actually such a box was needed to store and keep safe important papers such as property deeds, wills, letters, etc. Supposedly, this box was kept near the door so if there were a fire or other disaster, the box and its contents could be saved.

The age of these boxes can often be determined by the style of hinges. Hand-forged strap hinges indicate an early date. The lock mechanism also will help date the box. Boxes with their original finish are rare. Until recent times, when a collector found such a box, it was considered necessary to remove the old dirty finish and apply some new paint or shellac. The first box pictured is such an example. A previous owner sanded until the pins holding the strap hinges were exposed on the top of the lid. Any clues as to previous owners or origins were gone forever. The box is walnut, which would indicate it was made in America, but the wood is very thin, indicating European origin. Researchers believe that the majority of these boxes were brought to America by early settlers instead of being made here.

The construction of this oval bentwood cheese box is identical to the first example, 3" x 6" x 3". *Courtesy Dianne L. Burton.*

Could these round bentwood cheese boxes, constructed identically to the oval boxes, be by the same maker? Of the same age? The one on left is about 6" x 7". *Courtesy Dianne L. Burton.*

Bible box of nailed construction, walnut, ornate lock plate missing, 13" x 19" x 9", c. 1750, $300.

Interior view of original, hand-forged strap hinges held with pins rather than screws.

Close-up view of old rose head, hand forged nails. These nails are not an infallible sign of age — some restoration suppliers carry new ones in a number of sizes.

Probably American made, this Bible box is constructed of walnut. The paint and gilt appear to be very old if not original. The dovetails are large and crudely constructed. The base is original — many very old boxes have had the base replaced after it rotted out from damp and age, 12" x 23" x 11", c. 1740, $400.

An interior view shows the till on the right and replaced iron hinges. A till in a box of this type and age was used for storing coins and possibly jewelry.

Original, hand-forged iron handle. The light lines are marks of old jack-plane finishing. There was always a slight ridge, which can be felt running across the grain of the wood.

Black Ball Boxes

Many fraternal organizations have rituals which are known only to the members. One of these not so secret rituals is commonly called "blackballing." When prospective members are to be chosen, each voting member is given two marbles, one black and one white. Only one marble is to be dropped into the box provided. A white ball means yes, a black one, no. A black ball found in the box means automatic denial of membership. The person "blackballing" is unknown as the marbles are held and deposited so that no one can see which one has actually been dropped into the box. The boxes provided for this rather barbaric practice were generally made of fine woods such as mahogany and walnut and were elaborately decorated. Most of them have a sliding half-lid and a handle on one side.

The handle is also missing on this blackball box of pine with original finish, nailed construction, hinged lid, slide-out divider and ornate brass hinge (common, factory made box), 9" x 4-1/2" x 4", c. 1890, $60.

Mahogany blackball box with painted roses and a number on its lid, probably used by a sorority or other women's organization. The center divider slides up to reveal and release the marbles. The handle is missing, 5-1/2" x 10" x 3-3/4", c. 1880, $120.

Box with divider in raised position.

The primitive, nailed pine blackball box is obviously one of a kind, made by a "Sunday" craftsman, probably in the third quarter of the nineteenth century. It appears never to have had any finish or decoration, 13" x 4-1/4" x 3", $75.

Nailed-walnut blackball box, c. 1870, $85.

Blanket Chests

As the name implies, a blanket chest is a large, lidded box used to hold bedding and other linens. They were a common household item throughout the nineteenth century. Judging from the great number available today, most households must have had several. The early, elaborately painted and decorated chests were made for young women, especially among the Pennsylvania Dutch. They were part of the dowry and were referred to as dower chests. The woman's name and date of birth were commonly part of the decoration. Some immigrant chests resemble somewhat early bride's chests.

Blanket chests were made of various kinds of hardwoods and also pine and poplar. Most were dovetailed with the lid having applied molding around the edges. There was always a lock and a till (a compartment with a lid) near the top left side. Some tills had secret compartments which could be accessed by lifting the side piece. Most had bracket bases or turned feet. Miniature blanket chests were popular gifts judging from the number found today. Most miniatures are obviously presentation pieces, meant to hold trinkets or mementos. Blanket chests were nearly always painted by the maker or original owner. Some are quite elaborate, with stenciling or graining. Some have two or three drawers beneath the case. An unusual blanket chest is a tall cased piece with false drawers. The piece was constructed to resemble a dresser but was actually a chest with a lift-type lid. The front would be painted or incised to resemble a regular chest of drawers.

Unusual details on this cherry wood blanket chest include fine reeding around the lid and on the bracket base, double dovetailing, and elaborate turnings on the bracket-base feet, 16" x 38" x 21", c. 1840, $600.

Interior view of the walnut blanket chest shows the five-piece top, till with lid, and replaced hinges.

Walnut blanket chest with paneled front and lid, turned legs, and original finish, 37" x 18" x 22", c. 1850, $750. *Private collection.*

Pine blanket chest with original, dark green paint and a simple
bracket base, 37" x 18" x 18", c. 1860, $450. *Private collection.*

This chest with breadboard lid construction
never had a till.

Poplar wood blanket chest, refinished long ago, 40" x 17" x 22", c. 1850, $400.

Walnut blanket chest on turned legs with castors. The lid has cleated ends and it has the original key. Painted on the bottom is an Illinois name and address. c. 1860, $500.

A good example of a style of construction often seen in the Midwest — cherry paneled with breadboard ends and bun feet, c. 1860, $800. *Courtesy James Hunsley.*

Bread Boxes

The narrow tapered boxes pictured originated in Canada and northern Maine and probably date from the second half of the nineteenth century. They were used to store long, narrow bread loaves.

Pine bread box with original, grained finish, nailed construction, and hinged slant lid, 8-1/2" x 12-1/2" x 25", $160.

Bread box with original yellow and brown paint, pine, nailed construction, 8-3/4" x 10" x 33-1/2", $120.

Bride's Boxes

Many bride's boxes are similar or identical to the decorated band boxes described in a previous chapter. They might be a little larger and more elaborate and have the bride's name lettered on the side. These should not be confused with bride's chests or blanket chests. The bride's chests were large and often times elaborately grain-painted and decorated. These large chests were primarily found among the so-called Pennsylvania Dutch in Pennsylvania, Maryland and Virginia. Decorated bride's boxes are also found in Scandinavian-settled areas in the Midwest. The decoration on the box is called "rosemaling," which is a free-hand type of painting — not stenciling. Some ethnic groups and religious communities had their own unique customs connected with engagements and marriages.

The first boxes pictured are from the Mascoutah, Illinois, area. According to local lore, it was the custom for a young man to give his fiancee one of these boxes with something that had belonged to his mother inside (a handkerchief or a piece of jewelry). Mascoutah was settled in the mid-1850s by German immigrants. These boxes were made by local craftsmen.

A slight difference in details of construction could be attributable to different makers.

The top is one piece on the largest box in collection.

Five Mascoutah brides' boxes, of bentwood construction, with loose (not hinged) lids, and original finish, date to about 1860-1890, $300 each. *Courtesy collection of Darlene Lesicko.*

This pine bride's box has its original paint and decoration, a dome top, nailed construction, and lock, 5-1/2" x 10" x 5-1/2", c. 1840, $250.

The decorated lid of bride's box.

The interior of bride's box has a clean, almost unused appearance. Many old boxes are like this, proving that these little boxes were treasured by their original and successive owners.

Camphor (Wood) Boxes

Many boxes imported from the Orient, especially from China, were made of camphor, an evergreen wood with a pungent, aromatic fragrance which repelled moths and other insects. The chests were especially prized for storing clothing and linens. The wood has a grain similar to rosewood, but the aroma is distinctly different. Chests are the most common items found today, but there are also sewing boxes (sometimes fitted with ivory utensils), writing or lap desks, and trinket boxes of various kinds. See Liquor Chests for illustration of camphor wood.)

Candle Boxes

When candles were the only source of light, having a safe and handy storage box was important. Homemade candles were soft and easily bent so they had to be stored lying flat. Since they were made of beeswax and/or tallow, mice and other vermin were attracted to them. Most candle boxes are about 12 inches long with a sliding top rather than a hinged lid. The most desirable candle boxes are painted and decorated, indicating that they were gifts. The black painted one pictured has initials on one side — probably the recipient's.

With the advent of the kerosene lamp, these unique little boxes were no longer needed. Reproductions have been made. An old box that has held wax candles will have a faint odor of wax or tallow and the bottom may be somewhat greasy. Some elaborately decorated examples have sold for astronomical prices in recent years. Another type of candle box is the long hanging type. These are less common than the sliding-lid type and there is some doubt about whether these boxes were really made for storing candles.

Close-up of candle box top with name.

Painted and decorated sliding-lid candle boxes are the most sought after type. The decorations, initials on the side, and name on the top of this pine box are all old, all original, 8 3/4" x 12" x 5", c. 1840, $400.

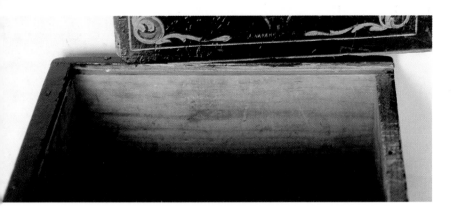

Interior showing nailed construction.

This sliding-lid candle box with compartments has an old grained finish on pine and nailed construction, 8-1/2" x 19" x 3-1/2", c.1850, $75.

There are unusual notches on three sides of this sliding-lid candle box with old finish, made of walnut with dovetailed construction, 9" x 11" x 4", c. l850, $200. *Private collection.*

Interior of box with compartments.

Sliding-lid, pine candle box, dovetailed, with old blue paint, c. 1860, $200.

This sliding-lid candle box is a rare construction of quarter-sawn maple, nailed, 12" x 4-1/8" x 8-3/4", c. 1850, $200. *Courtesy James Hunsley.*

A cellarette on removable stand made of mahogany with pine interiors. Features a pull-out tray and dovetailed drawer, original brasses and intact lock mechanism. Many cellarettes have metal handles on the sides, unlike this one, c. 1800, $800.

The interior of this cellarette has nine compartments.

Cellarettes

Cellarette is a twentieth-century term for a lidded box on a stand used to store bottles of wine and liquor. The box was always made of fine wood such as mahogany or walnut. The interior was fitted with wooden partitions, generally twelve or sixteen. Some boxes had handles on the sides. There was always a lock. The table upon which the box sat generally had a slide-out mixing tray and a drawer. The early boxes are rectangular, but later Empire-style ones were eight-sided and sometimes lined in zinc. They were considered part of the dining room furnishings and later examples were made to match the dining room "set." Small portable liquor boxes fitted with bottles and glasses were called "tantalus" and had a device to lock the decanters in place

Chip Carved Boxes

Chip carving, as its name implies, is a process of embellishing a plain surface by gouging out small slivers of wood to form a design. It is a form of folk art similar to its successor, tramp art. Fine hardwoods were generally used. The practice seems to have died out by 1870.

This letter box is chip carved on three sides with brass locks, 7-1/4" x 9-1/2" x 4", c. 1850, $125.

Chip-carved document box opens from the side and has a lock mechanism. Made of butternut or walnut, 10-3/4" x 15-1/2" x 4-1/2", c. 1850, $250.

Chip-carved, four-drawer miniature chest of walnut, c. 1850, $650. *Courtesy collection of Darlene Lesicko.*

Top of chip-carved box.

Coin Boxes (Banks)

When banks are mentioned, almost everyone thinks of cast iron in the shape of animals or buildings. Banks were made from a variety of other materials including tin, plaster, glass, pottery, and wood. Wood banks were nearly always simple, rectangular boxes with a slot in the top and, of course, a lock. Some were cut to resemble a chest of drawers with little knobs and turned feet. Some were carved in the shape of fruit such as a pear or an apple. These coin boxes could have been used in other ways besides encouraging children to save. The larger ones could have been used in churches, either as alms boxes or to gather collections. Fraternal and other organizations could also have used them. It is not surprising to find most have a damaged or broken lock.

Simple, pine-box bank with slot in lid. Originally it had leather hinges; the lock mechanism is intact, with old finish, c. 1860, $100.

Cylindrical bank of soft wood, old red paint, c. 1880, $35. *Private collection.*

Comb Cases

Comb cases, like soap boxes, were simple, nailed, hanging boxes used in country kitchens and on back porches. A few of them were attached to a small rectangular framed mirror. Occasionally an elaborate carved or decorated version is found. These were probably meant for bedroom use.

Unique, walnut comb case of nailed construction, 8" long, c. 1870, $75. *Private collection.*

Pine comb case of nailed construction, 9" x 11" x 3-3/4", c. 1890, $75. *Courtesy collection of Darlene Lesicko.*

A factory made, nailed oak comb case, 1890, $35.

Pine, nailed comb case with shelf and heart-shaped cutout, c. 1880, $250. *Courtesy collection of Darlene Lesicko.*

German influence is evidenced in this pineapple-motif, chip-carved comb case of walnut, with original finish, c. 1870, $75. *Courtesy James Hunsley.*

A pine comb case, nailed, with old paint, 8" x 4-1/2" x 2-3/4", c. 1880, $75. *Courtesy collection of Darlene Lesicko.*

Compartmented Boxes

Boxes in this category were made to hold small items or collections. The original purpose of the compartments is lost, creating intrigue and mystery. Not included in this category are boxes whose original purpose is obvious, such as jewelry or stamp storage.

Mahogany with satinwood inlay box has a lift-out, seventeen-compartment tray and a brass lock with ivory escutcheon, 9" x 13" x 5", c. 1840, $250.

Interior, red paint on the lid is original.

This mahogany veneer box has a seven-compartment, lift-out tray
and brass lock, 8-1/2" x 12" x 4-3/4", c. 1845, $175.

This box also has compartments beneath its
tray, c. 1840, $150.

Mahogany and satinwood inlay box with ivory escutcheon, brass lock, 11" x 7-1/2" x 4-1/2", c. l835, $250.

Interior of box with 12-compartment, lift-out tray.

Plain walnut box with velvet-lined dividers and brass lock, 5-1/2" x
8" x 4", c. 1860, $75.

Interior of box that probably held bottles.

Original blue paint coats this compartmented, dovetailed box with lock, 12" x 17-3/4" 6-1/2", c. l860, $250. *Courtesy collection of Darlene Lesicko.*

Interior of box.

Compartmented walnut box, dovetailed, with brass lock and original finish, 15-3/4" x 10-7/8" x 5", c. 1850, $350. *Courtesy James Hunsley.*

Open box with three hinges.

Compartmented cherry wood box, dovetailed, with original finish and lock, 18-3/4" x 9-1/4" x 9-1/2", c. 1850, $350. *Courtesy James Hunsley.*

Open box with divider visible on left, fine dovetailing.

Compartmented box with original, putty colored paint, dovetailed, no lock, 14" x 18", c. l850, $395. *Courtesy collection of Darlene Lesicko.*

Open box showing dividers.

Cutlery Boxes

Cutlery boxes and knife boxes are some times confused. A cutlery box is a two-compartment, open box with a cut-out handle. They were used to store and carry tableware from the pantry to the dining area. Most of them have slanted sides, are constructed with nails, and are made from soft wood such as pine or poplar. They are being reproduced.

The bottom should be one piece of wood. There should be signs of wear and stains. If it looks "too nice" it's probably of recent manufacture. Knife boxes are rectangular or round storage and display boxes found only in the homes of the wealthy. See Knife Boxes for more information.

Pine cutlery box with canted sides and one-piece, cut-out handle, nailed, 8" x 11" x 5", c. 1880, $40.

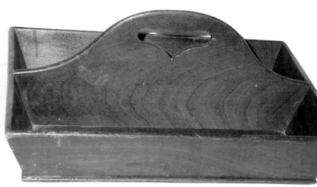

Pine cutlery box with old, orange-shellac finish and brass handle. What appears to be wood graining is actually paint. Probably factory-made, 8-1/2" x 12" x 2", c. 1900, $40.

An unusually high divider gives this nailed-walnut cutlery box distinction, along with canted sides and heart-shape cutout handhold, 13" x 9-1/2" x 6", c. 1880, $125. *Private collection.*

Maple and cherry veneered cutlery box with three compartments, damaged handle, 8" x 14" x 2-1/2", c. 1880, $75.

Nailed-pine cutlery box with old finish, 13" x 7-1/2" x 5", c. 1880, $95. *Private collection.*

The hinged lids appear to be a later addition to this nailed cutlery box, but the original blue-grey paint on pine is the same, c. 1880, $200.

The one-piece bottom of this box shows evidence of wear, square nails.

An unusual finger-grip handle marks this nailed-walnut cutlery box with canted sides, 9" x 13" x 4-1/2" c. 1880, $200. *Courtesy collection of Darlene Lesicko.*

Nailed-pine cutlery box with original green paint, 14-1/2" x 9-1/2" x 6", c. 1880, $250. *Courtesy collection of Darlene Lesicko.*

Cutlery box with mustard-over-green paint, nailed, canted sides, 9-3/4" x 13" x 4", $120. *Courtesy collection of Darlene Lesicko.*

Nailed-pine cutlery box with original blue paint, 10" x 14" x 6-1/2", c. 1880, $230. *Courtesy collection of Darlene Lesicko.*

Walnut cutlery box with original finish, cast-brass handle, dovetailed, 8-1/2" x 11-3/4" x 4-1/8", c. 1880, $300. *Courtesy James Hunsley.*

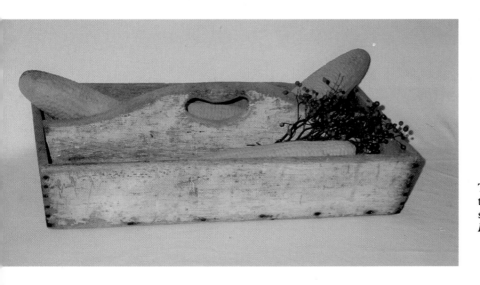

Traces of original white paint remain on this nailed-pine cutlery box with canted sides, c. 1890, $125. *Courtesy collection of Darlene Lesicko.*

Nailed-pine cutlery box with original paint, c. 1890, $150. *Courtesy collection of Darlene Lesicko.*

Nailed cutlery box with scrubbed finish. c. 1885, $195. *Courtesy collection of Darlene Lesicko.*

Decorated Boxes (Painted)

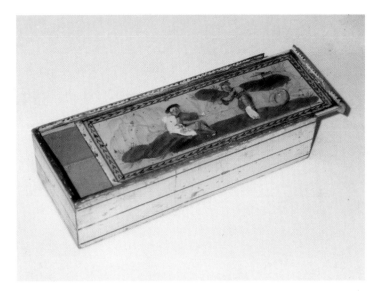

Mitered pine box is paint and gesso decorated on top with painted and striped sides, and painted bright blue inside, 3-1/2" x 9" x 2-1/2", c. 1820-1830, $200.

There is probably a paint-decorated box for almost every category covered in this book. One popular style is schoolgirl art, which is generally more theorem-like than original. The teacher would tell the pupils what they were to paint. Some, of course, were more talented than others. Some "Sunday" painters were totally self-taught. A young man would be moved to create something useful and beautiful for his intended. Often paint was applied to hide the fact that the item was made of several different kinds of wood, a cover-up more often found in furniture than boxes). Sailors would use ivory or whalebone for decorative inlay. Occasionally, they would use silver coins rolled into thin wire for inlay along with nacre (mother-of-pearl). Rarely one finds a box in which different kinds of wood are dyed and cut into stars or other decorative inlays. In the last years of the nineteenth century, a decorating craze called pyrography was practiced in all parts of the country. A heated stylus was used to burn a design into soft wood such as pine. Very few who practiced this craft used original designs. Patterns could be purchased from women's magazines.

Paint- and paper-decorated pine box has a slide top and lapped joints, 4-1/2" x 6-3/4" x 4-1/4", c. 1830, $35.

Painted scene appears to be a school or factory on a nailed pine, slide-top box. Naive in style, it is a true folk piece, 5-1/4" x 8" x 4", pre-1840, $400. *Courtesy collection of Darlene Lesicko.*

View of top

Original red paint covers this nailed-pine box, which was probably used for documents and includes a lock and a narrow yellow stripe around the top, 10" x 14-3/4" x 6-3/4", c. 1860, $150.

Box top has an iron plate and handle.

Yellow and ochre, grain-painted pine box is rabbeted and has a brass bail (handle) on its lid, 7-1/4" x 10" x 4-1/2", c. 1850, $95.

44

Detail of graining on lid, probably done with a coarse comb.

Original red paint with gold-stenciled deer motif graces the lid and front of this nailed-pine box with lock, 6" x 10-1/2" x 5", c. 1870, $150.

The top of the box has a black band and yellow stripes.

Faux-oak, paint-grained box may have held decorator's samples. It has different styles of graining on the top, sides and inside; pine, nailed, 9" x 15-3/4" x 7-1/4", c. 1890, $80.

Open box shows different styles of graining.

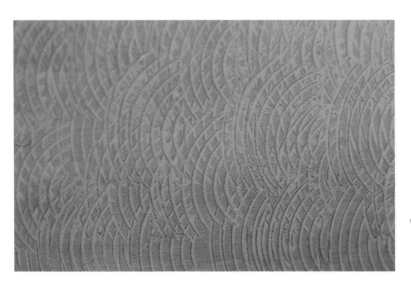

Close-up of graining design on inside of lid.

Original red paint with a painted, not lithographed, Currier and Ives-type picture on the lid; pine, nailed, with lock, 7-3/4" x 13" x 5", c. 1890, $110.

Pine box painted orange, yellow and red on four sides and top; hinged with lock, 13" x 15" x 9", c. 1845, $225. *Private collection.*

Miniature, dome-top pine box has original naive scene on all sides and top; hinged with lock, c. 1830, $225. *Private collection.*

Paint-decorated, nailed-pine box, missing lid, 12" x 12" x 12", c. 1830, $120. *Private collection.*

A stencil of nude figure holds what appears to be a pipe on this paint-decorated pine box with divider. Painted red with yellow and brown stripes, the pine wood has been serrated, 8" x 4-1/2" x 3-1/2", c. 1890, $25.

Box painted to resemble walnut with yellow and black banding, as well as painted green leaves and a flower on the lid, 10" x 7-1/4" x 4", c. 1880, $95.

Decorated Boxes (Inlay Work)

Inlay is a process of cutting small pieces of various woods and arranging them to form a pattern generally geometric. Inlay boxes can be divided into two distinct categories — sophisticated work done by skilled artisans either working alone or in small factories and naive attempts by someone just wanting to make something "pretty." The later falls under the category of folk art as almost all were made by self-taught tinkerers and are one of a kind.

Intricate shapes are obviously more difficult to work with than rectangular shapes, as witnessed by this walnut with satinwood inlay box with lock, done by someone with skill. The pattern is a mariner's star, a popular motif throughout the nineteenth century, c. 1840, $650. *Private collection.*

A lady's trinket box with interior tray has heart-shaped pincushions inside and a cards and games motif of mahogany, rosewood, and satinwood on the exterior, 8" x 12" x 4-1/2", c. 1840, $300.

Inside, the lift-out tray is also veneered, with space between the hearts for storing a thimble.

Paint and various inlaid hardwoods were used to create a mariner's star and circle motif on three sides and the top of this nailed-pine box, 7" x 12" x 4", c. 1840, $150.

Lid of box.

Only the dark walnut pieces on this pine box are inlay; the rest of the design is created with paint. Rabbeted with lock, 9" x 12" x 4", c. 1860, $100.

The dark dots around the lid's rim appear to be nails but are actually small inlay circles.

Document Boxes

Document boxes were the successors to Bible boxes. They are smaller than Bible boxes and some are fitted with a removable tray, have a handle on the top, and are decorated with inlay work of contrasting wood. They are a marked contrast to their cousins made of tin and painted with a tole design. The wooden boxes were obviously more expensive and many were probably made in England or on the Continent. The most beautiful ones date from the beginning of the nineteenth century. After about 1840, most document boxes were made of rosewood, which was also the favored wood for high-styled Victorian furniture. Instead of elaborate inlay, the decoration was often a band of coin silver around the edges of the top of the lid with a simple mother-of-pearl key hole surround. Document boxes were also made by itinerant craftsmen. They are generally plain and sturdy, well-made with dovetailed construction, and often painted.

Indications of early construction are the small, finely executed dovetailing, the "platform" base and the ornate lock escutcheon on this walnut, dovetailed box with beveled-edge lid, original brass handle, and side drawer with no lock, 6" x 12" x 6-1/2", c. 1830, $200.

This box, like nearly all document boxes, has no interior fittings or partitions, but it has original key. It is constructed of rosewood veneer arranged in a triangle design with a slightly canted top, 9" x 13" x 5-3/4", c. 1850, $150.

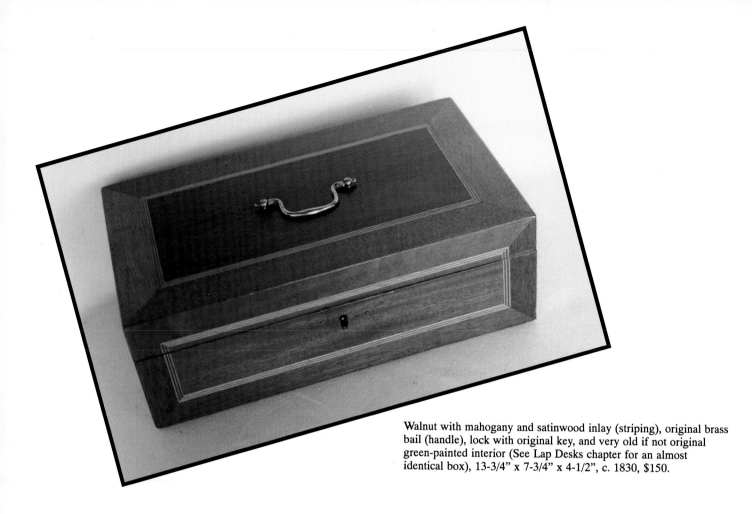

Walnut with mahogany and satinwood inlay (striping), original brass bail (handle), lock with original key, and very old if not original green-painted interior (See Lap Desks chapter for an almost identical box), 13-3/4" x 7-3/4" x 4-1/2", c. 1830, $150.

Pine box, dovetailed with original brass bail (handle) and original key, 9" x 14" x 6-1/2", c.1850, $110.

Inlay on all four sides of cherry and curly maple veneer, along with a brass lock, mortise and tenon, 13-3/4" x 8-1/4" x 4-2/3", c.1840, $200.

Mahogany veneer over pine; dovetailed with lock, 9" x 13-1/2" x 6", c. 1840, $75.

Original dark red paint decorates pine box with removable tray and lock; rabbeted, 9" x 16" x 7-1/2", c.1850, $120.

Removable tray with partition.

Exotic wood, burled, with satinwood inlay over pine, 10" x 14" x 4", c. 1850, $90.

Exotic wood veneer; with lock, 8-1/2" x 12" x 5", c. 1850, $80.

Flat, one-piece top, walnut, dovetailed, with lock. 8-1/4" x 12" x 5", c. 1860, $130.

Possibly a document box, this pine dovetailed construction has its original finish; no lock, c. 1850, $80.

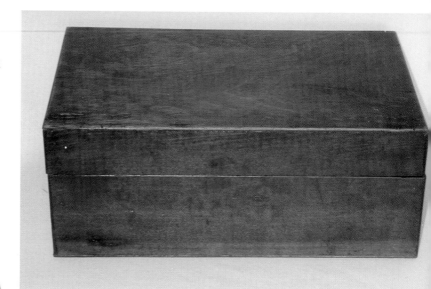

Interior view of pine box.

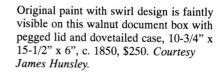

Original paint with swirl design is faintly visible on this walnut document box with pegged lid and dovetailed case, 10-3/4" x 15-1/2" x 6", c. 1850, $250. *Courtesy James Hunsley.*

Dome Top Boxes

All sorts of storage boxes were made with dome tops, but the best known ones are the trunks seen atop stage coaches in Western movies. Supposedly the dome top was a primitive form of water proofing. Many immigrant's trunks had domed tops. When they were stacked in ships' holds, the dome tops kept them from sliding about. Each trunk acted as a wedge for the one next to it. The domed top was also popular for a time for tea caddies and other small boxes. The dome top trunks were generally made of soft wood. All were painted and some were grained to resemble more exotic woods. All had locks. Occasionally a trunk will be found with its original wallpaper or fabric lining. These domed trunks should not be confused with the later domed style trunks sold by Sears and Montgomery Ward.

Dome-top trunk was originally painted red over pine; pegged and nailed, with lock, 12" x 29" x 12-1/2", c. 1850, $100.

Dome-top, nailed-pine box with original dark brown paint, 11-1/2" x 6-1/2" x 7", $150. *Courtesy collection of Darlene Lesicko.*

Interior of what may have been a bride's box, with initials JBM, dated 1868.

This box, dated to early 1850, presents its owner with a dilemma: The date on the side, 1838, is obviously not genuine. Should one leave this as is or attempt to strip it down to the original paint? Nailed with brass hasp, 8" x 6" x 8".

Dough Boxes

In the days when bread was made at home, almost every housewife had a dough box. It was not, as the name suggests, a place to store bread. Rather, kneaded dough was placed in the box to rise. The sides and lid protected the rising dough from drafts and sudden shifts in temperature. Some bread dough (notably white) was punched down after the first rising, shaped into loaves and allowed to rise again. The entire process was time consuming, so a dough box freed up space for other kitchen tasks. Many dough boxes sat on a frame of four canted legs. The boxes themselves were dovetailed, had slanted sides, and a loose lid (no hinges). With the lid in place, the box top could serve as a work surface.

An overly zealous refinisher has succeeded in removing almost all signs of age and use in this pine dough box, which is mortised on the sides with cutout handholds shaped like hearts and a cleated top, 14" x 35" x 12", c. 1850, $250.

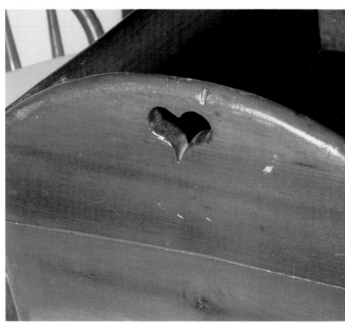

The bottom of a dough box showing signs of age and use. This box obviously never had a stand or frame, as the deep scratches indicate.

Heart-shaped, cutout handholds

Dower Chest

The dower chest was considered part of the dowry or marriage portion that a bride brought with her to her new home. This was a custom practiced by the Germans and Scandinavians who brought the tradition with them from their homeland. The dower chest was an elaborately decorated, large blanket chest. Some had drawers in the base. Experts can tell what county or region a chest came from by its construction and decoration. Often the bride's name was incorporated into the decoration as in the example pictured.

Pennsylvania German bride's chest with original paint and decoration; name and date — "Johanna Gebbart D.D. April 1824;" constructed of pine with original strap hinges; lock mechanism missing, 25" x 48" x 18-1/2", $800.

Detail of original grain painting, no over paint or touchup.

Soap Hollow bride's chest with grain paint over pine. The finish and decor are all original. Name on the front is "Eve Most," born in Somerset, Pennsylvania, 1828, married in 1887. Possibly it was her second marriage. Dated 1850, the maker's initials are J.K. (Koffman?), 50" x 23" x 32", $4,500. *Courtesy collection of Darlene Lesicko.*

Soap Hollow is the name given to a distinctive style of furniture made in Somerset County, Pennsylvania, by Amish and Mennonite craftsmen between 1843 and 1900. There were eight listed in various census records. The furniture is painted and decorated in a distinctive, recognizable style. For more information, see "Manufactured by Hand, The Soap Hollow School, Southern Alleghenies Museum of Art, Loretto, Pennsylvania," a catalog issued by the museum, copyright 1993.

Dressing Boxes

Dressing or vanity boxes were made for both men and women. Their chief identifying characteristic is the mirror inside the lid. There is generally a lift-out tray with compartments. The compartments were fitted with bottles and jars or were lidded. The wood used was generally mahogany or rosewood. A few boxes were made with a hinged, framed mirror that could be adjusted to catch the light. Most appear to have been made in the first half of the nineteenth century.

Lady's dressing box with mahogany veneer over pine with satinwood inlay and ivory escutcheon, 6-1/2" x 10-1/2" x 4", c. 1830, $200.

Interior of box showing five satinwood and mahogany lids plus velvet pincushion, mirror in lid, and lock mechanism. Tray lifts out.

A lady's dressing box fitted with bottles, five lidded compartments, velvet lining (original), and mahogany veneer with silver plate and escutcheon, 13" x 9" x 5", c. 1835, $175.

Interior of box. Bottles may be original.

Inscribed "Mrs. Babcock of Charlestown," this lady's dressing box is of mahogany veneer with coin silver plaque on lid, locks, and ivory escutcheons. The four ball feet may not be original, 13-1/2" x 9" x 4-1/2", c. 1810, $300.

Interior of box — the mirror is intact but the fittings are gone.

A man's dressing box features coin silver and rosewood banding, mahogany veneer, and key. The mirror is in the lid, but the interior fittings are gone. c. 1840, $140.

A mirror swings from hinges attached to the front of this box's lid. Framed in rosewood veneer, it rests on a ledge on inside front of box. This is an uncommon design — most of these mirrors probably broke and were discarded long ago.

Satinwood veneered box with dark wood inlay and lock with ornate escutcheon, 5-1/2" x 7-1/4" x 3", c. 1880, $75.

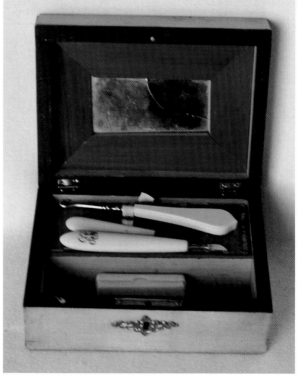

The fittings inside the box are not original. The handles on the implements are ivorene — a forerunner of celluloid.

This pine dressing box with rosewood veneer could have belonged to a man or woman. The interior fittings are gone. It is decorated with coin silver banding, inlay, and escutcheon, (coin silver turns yellow rather than black and appears to be brass until cleaned) and lock, c. 1840, $90 as is.

An interior view shows a mirror with ornate frame. Interiors were often painted with red and black graining to resemble rosewood.

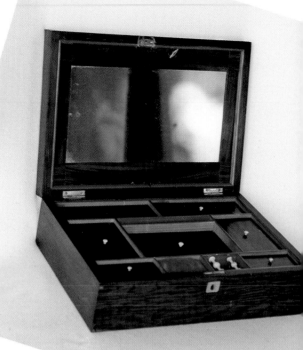

Rosewood veneer on this pine dressing box is similar to previous example, with coin silver banding and plate, 9" x 12-1/2" x 4" inches, c. 1850, $200.

The interior of this box has a mirror with ornate frame and eight compartments, seven of them with grain-painted lids, ivory knobs, and two carved ivory thread winders.

The drawer on this flame mahogany veneered box was kept closed and locked by a long brass rod visible in the second picture The interior fittings and mirror in lid may be original, c. 1810, $150.

Fourteen small compartments fill this box, three of them large, two with lids. The bun feet are original.

64

Rosewood veneer dressing box with curly maple interior, ivory escutcheon, wavy beading around base and top, 10" x 16-3/4" x 7", c. 1840, $300.

Open box with mirror covered shows ornate maple, not paint. The tray lifts out.

This mirror has a cover which may also have functioned as a tray. Partitions are visible beneath lid cover.

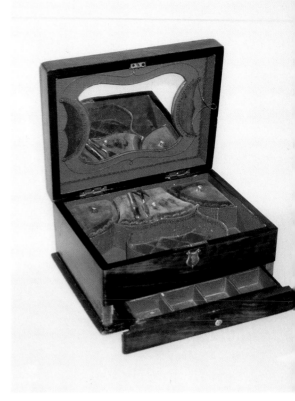

This late-nineteenth century lady's dressing box has original fittings, $110.

Open box with mirror and lidded compartments.

Box open in first position.

Dressing box with black paint on pine, gold stenciling, mirror in lid, purple velvet and purple paper liner, 8" x 11-3/4" x 5-1/2", c. 1860, $100.

Box with folding flap in open position, partition missing.

Game Boxes

Elaborate inlaid boxes were made specifically to hold pieces for games such as backgammon. Sometimes the boxes were part of the game set, as in the example pictured. In the early nineteenth century, elaborate lacquered boxes with ivory game pieces were brought to America on Clipper Ships. Some boxes were made by skilled or semiskilled tinkers or "Sunday craftsmen." Checker boxes are the most common example. A checkerboard was inlaid or painted into the top and bottom of the box, which could be opened out to use as a playing board. In the later years of the nineteenth century, toy companies made boxes with lithographed designs to hold game pieces. Cribbage boards were also boxes.

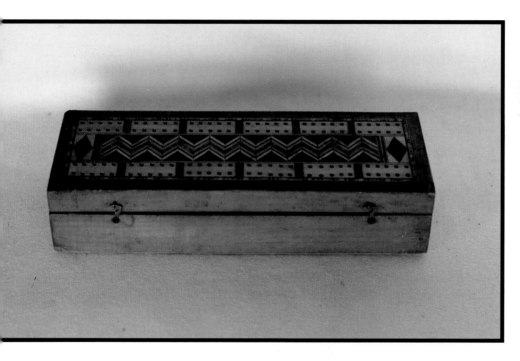

A walnut cribbage box with satinwood inlay, game pieces missing. Cribbage was a gambling type game, played with dies and pegs,
4-1/2" x 11-1/2" x 2-1/2", 1880, $20.

Top view of box showing holes for pegs.

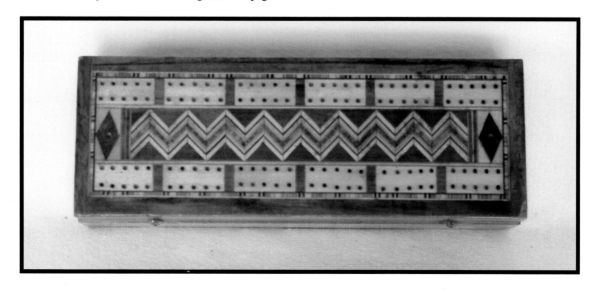

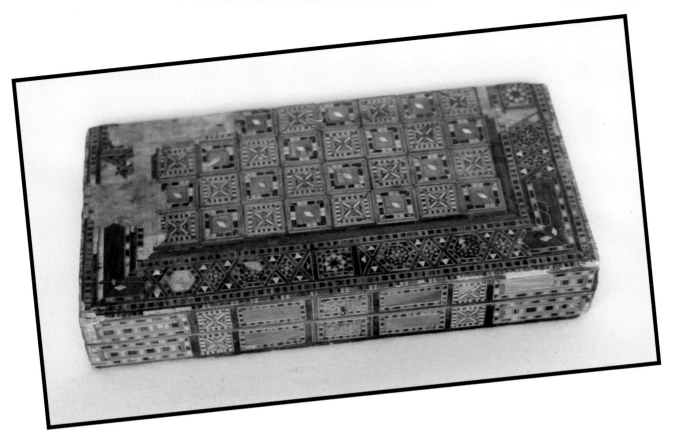

Backgammon box with exotic wood inlay, in need of extensive
repair, game pieces missing. Early nineteenth century, $50 as is.

Interior of backgammon box. When opened this way, the board was
ready for a game of backgammon; when opened and turned upside
down, the box could be used for chess.

A walnut game box with lift off lid and brass corners and trim.
Probably for mahjong, a game played with tiles and dice, 9" x
11-1/4" x 4-1/2", probably very late nineteenth century, $40.

Box has drawer on side, lift-off
lid, banded and brass trimmed.

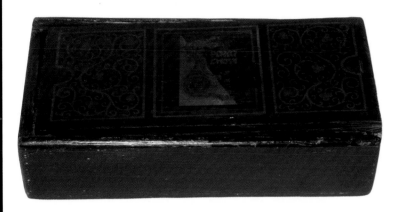

Game box with ivory counters and two dice, slide top, black paint with scroll decorations, rabbeted construction. Game is called Pang Chow, possibly the same as mahjong, 5-3/4" x 11" x 2-1/4", 1890 or later, $40.

Box with counters and dice.

Grain Measuring Boxes

Grain Measuring boxes are round, lidless containers used in mills and grain elevators. The law required them to be accurate (to insure the honesty of the mill operators). They were sized by dry measure — bushel, peck, half peck, etc. The wood was generally pine, sometimes painted. The most desirable items have the name of the elevator or mill stamped on the side.

This set of four measures with original blue paint was once used in a grain elevator in Edwardsville, Illinois, c. 1890, $400. *Courtesy collection of Darlene Lesicko.*

Boxes turned upside down to show details of construction.

Humidors

Most humidors date from the last half of the nineteenth century. The majority are simple, rectangular boxes lined with glass. They were used to store cigars or tobacco. The glass lining supposedly kept the cigars moist. Most are made of walnut or mahogany, have no inlay or other decoration, and no lock. They are common and generally found in good condition. These boxes are not highly prized since there are so many of them and they are all so similar. An exception is the round or barrel shaped humidor often made from exotic wood. Also unusual are boxes inscribed with a gift recipient's name and date.

A humidor of rosewood with satinwood inlay and lock, glass lined, resembles a tea caddy. It was probably used for loose tobacco or cigarillos (cigarettes would not come into general use until the end of the century), 4-1/2" x 5-3/4" x 4", c. 1850, $75.

Interior of humidor with opaque glass lining in lid. The glass was removed from the sides, probably broken long ago.

A common, late humidor, has plate in lid for inscribing. Mahogany, painted black band, 9" x 12" x 3" inches, c. 1900, $25.

Interior of box, tin lined.

A novelty humidor, this may have been a souvenir from a resort. It is supposed to resemble logs, and is fastened together with pegs and stained dark. Pine with lock, mortise and tenon, 6" x 11-1/4" 4", c. l880, $35.

Interior of box, painted with "silver paint" over paper.

Cylindrical humidor made of lignum vitae, a hard, dense wood from Central America. Four pieces and a removable silver plate liner, the base screws into the case, 6-1/2" x 5", c. 1870, $90.

Oak humidor, engine turnings, has silver plate liner, 4-1/2" tall without lid, 4" diameter, c. 1885, $50.

Interior of humidor.

Immigrants Trunks

The first settlers undoubtedly brought with them only what they could carry. There was little or no room on the ship for anything but the necessities, which were often held in common. There are no surviving examples of the earliest immigrant chests. Later, in the eighteenth and also the nineteenth century, immigrants from northern Europe often brought all their belongings including tools and household utensils in a large, slant-sided, sometimes domed-top wooden trunk. The traveler's name and destination would be painted on the side in large letters, including the words Nord Amerika or U.S.A. The plain, undecorated trunks are of little interest to most collectors, but some have survived and are treasured by the descendants of the original owners. The elaborately painted and decorated examples are starting to attract more attention as people become aware of their "roots" and seek some connection with their forebears.

A rare immigrants trunk with original rosemaling (a type of decoration practiced by Scandinavians), this trunk could have been a bride's chest originally. Made of soft wood, it has a dome top and is reinforced on the outside corners and also inside. The name of the owner and destination is painted on the back, 40" x 20" x 19", c. 1850 $700. *Courtesy Rees Antiques on the Square, Carlinville, Illinois.*

Painting on the front is in very good condition, details intact.

The words "immigrant" and "Illinois" are decipherable, the others aren't. There are reinforcement bands on the right and in the center.

An immigrant's pine trunk with strap hinges (again, probably originally a bride or dower chest), shows traces of rosemaling visible beneath later paint. Scandinavian origin, brought to America in mid-nineteenth century, 48" x 24" x 20", c. 1820, $900. *Private collection.*

The trunk's till with a secret compartment, revealed by raising a dark brown panel.

An immigrant's trunk with original paint and decorations. Metal reinforcing bands around the corner indicate that this trunk was probably not new when it was prepared for its journey to the United States in the mid-nineteenth century, 52" x 22" x 17-1/2", $900. *Courtesy collection of Darlene Lesicko.*

Jewelry Boxes

If a collector were interested in acquiring the greatest number of boxes covering the longest span of time, jewelry boxes would be a good choice. They range from crude little slide-top boxes to elaborate ivory, brass, silver, and exotic-wood inlay mahogany or rosewood. The larger ones have a removable partitioned tray. The entire box is often lined in velvet or silk. There is generally a slotted compartment for rings. A few have secret compartments. Often the original owner's initials are engraved on a silver or ivory panel set in the lid.

Box interior has slots for rings or earrings. It may have had a mirror in its lid originally.

Lady's jewel box of rosewood with brass inlay, ivory plate, escutcheon, original silk lining, ripple molding, and lock, 6-1/2" x 9" x 3-3/4", c. 1840, $75.

Though this mahogany jewelry box with chip carving, brass inlay and brass lock is old, new boxes with similar carvings and mother-of-pearl inlay are coming into the country by the hundreds (see chapter on reproductions), 8" x 12" x 3-1/4", c. 1880, $80.

Box with mirror in lid, green silk, and dark blue velvet lining. Tray lifts out.

Soft wood is covered with fabric and paper to make a presentation box with the jeweler's name inside. Paper and decor all original. Late nineteenth Century, $40. *Courtesy Diane M. Dudley, Yesterday's Market and Chicken Coop.*

Box open showing two compartments, the lower lined in bright blue silk.

Box with sliding cases open.

A pine jewel box with old dark finish and carved flower design on lid. Two boxes slide out to reveal storage space beneath. Lined in original purple paper with milk glass ball feet, lock, mortise and tenon, 6" x 6" x 5" inches, c. 1880, $45.

Knife Boxes

"Knife box" is the generally used term for the elaborate, lidded mahogany boxes used by the wealthy in the eighteenth and early nineteenth century to display and store silver-handled knives. They were always made in pairs and were displayed on the sideboard in the dining room. There were two distinct styles, the earlier boxes were rectangular with a slanted lid. There were slots near the top to hold the silver and to keep the pieces from being scratched. Later the rounded pedestal urn-type box became popular. The conical shaped lids were not hinged but were raised and removed by means of a center rod. These boxes were reproduced during and after the centennial era. Most of the early ones were made in England. A careful analysis of the wood is required to establish age and origin. The early rectangular types had locks.

Mahogany knife box with silver escutcheon, mariner's star inlay in lid, original key. Slots for the knives are missing, c. 1780, $500.

Lap Desks
(See also, Writing Boxes)

Anyone who has ever been curious about or collected lap desks will notice the lack of information about them in the standard reference books. They are mentioned briefly, if at all, which seems odd since so many have survived. Almost every shop or mall which purports to carry "real" antiques will have several. The most famous lap desk extant is the one often seen in photos of Thomas Jefferson's bedroom- study. It was on this desk that the Declaration of Independence was drafted and revised.

Basically a lap desk is a rectangular, hinged, lidded box with two flat writing surfaces level with the top of the box and the edge of the lid. The lid is cut at an angle to form a slanting surface. When in use, the box is turned so that the lid is closest to the body. There are compartments in the front base of the box to hold ink bottles and pens. Many lap desks have secret compartments. Some have a drawer in the base which opens from the side. (If it opened from the front, the drawer would not be accessible when the box was in use.) There is also storage space behind the writing surface of the lid.

The larger boxes were made for men and generally were bound or trimmed in brass. Boxes made for women or schoolgirls often had elaborate inlay of silver, mother-of-pearl, and exotic woods. The inside was painted white. Miniatures are known. Early examples are one-of-a-kind. Many are similar but no two are exactly alike. Late examples are mass produced (machine-made). They can be found in early Sears and Montgomery Ward catalogs. They are simple boxes without drawers or secret compartments. Many of the early ones were made in England. Lap desks were also imported from China and India.

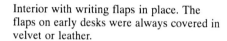

A man's lap desk of mahogany veneer with ivory escutcheon, and lock. The interior fittings not original, ll-1/2" x 17" x 8", c. 1810, $200.

Interior with writing flaps in place. The flaps on early desks were always covered in velvet or leather.

A man's lap desk, mahogany with brass bands and a full-length drawer that opens from the side. The interior is intact and all original, 11" x 21" x 7", c. 1810, $300.

A locking device for a drawer — the brass rod slid into a hole drilled through the case and the drawer front. When the brass rod was in place, the drawer could not be opened, note old ink stain in drawer, an indication of age.

Case open in correct position for use, compartments for pens and ink are at top. Flap in lid can be lifted to access paper.

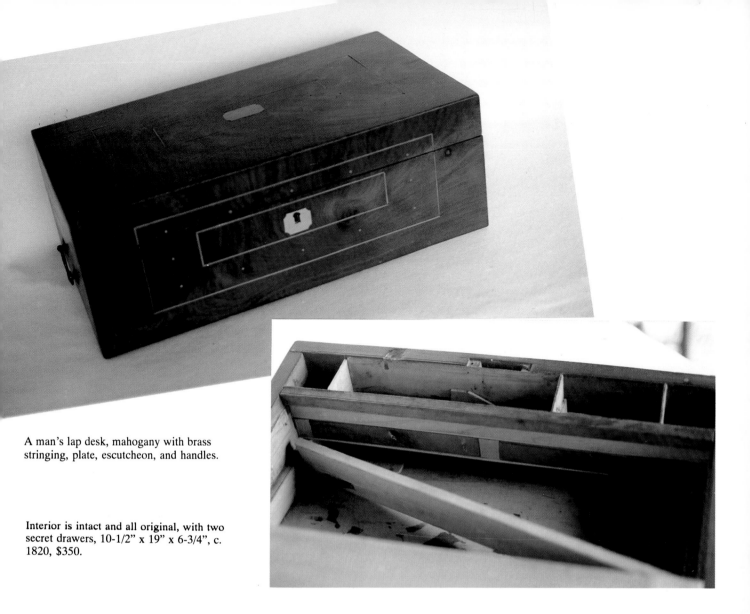

A man's lap desk, mahogany with brass stringing, plate, escutcheon, and handles.

Interior is intact and all original, with two secret drawers, 10-1/2" x 19" x 6-3/4", c. 1820, $350.

A lady's lap desk of rosewood with floral decor of coin silver and mother-of-pearl. The interior fittings are gone, the inside painted white (original), 14-1/2" x 10" x 8-1/2", c. 1840, $75.

A lady's or schoolgirl's lap desk of rosewood with coin silver and mother-of-pearl fittings mostly intact, inside painted white. Some silver is missing around the edge of the lid, 14-3/4" x 10" x 5-1/4", c. 1840, $125.

Interior of desk with flaps up, white paint original.

Lady's lap desk of rosewood with coin silver and mother-of- pearl, interior intact with two original ink bottles. Top needs extensive repair. Lid edge design is slightly different from previous example, 9" x 13" x 5", c. 1840, $90.

Similar to two previous examples, this rosewood box has coin silver and mother-of-pearl embellishments and its interior fittings partly intact. It needs extensive repairs, 15" x 10-1/4" x 5", c. 1940, $75.

This lady's lap desk has exotic wood veneer, silver and mother-of-pearl inlay. The center part of the top is not original. The interior is partly intact, 9-1/4" x 13" x 5", c. 1840, $65.

This man's lap desk of rosewood has brass-bound corners, brass bands, plate, and escutcheon. The interior is intact and it has the original key, 8-3/4" x 13-3/4" x 4-3/4", c. 1830, $200.

Interior of desk with original bottles.

A man's lap desk of solid walnut with incised carving; interior intact, 13" x 8-3/4" x 5", c. 1860, $125.

Interior with original purple velvet covering, elaborate borders on flaps.

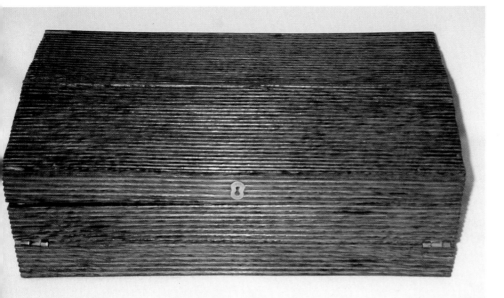

Lap desk of exotic, oak-type wood, reeded top and front, opens into three sections with all interior fittings intact. It probably was imported from the Orient, 8-3/4" x 15" x 5", c. 1840, $300.

Desk open to first position, no flap in lid, racks for storing booklets or papers.

Desk open completely, third part opens to form writing surface.

Three secret drawers hidden behind ruler-like slat. Dowel rod is part of fittings, possibly used as a paper weight.

A lady's walnut lap desk has original finish, floral design painted on top, yellow striping. The interior is intact with two ink bottles, 8-3/4" x 12" x 3", c. 1870, $120.

Lap desk of rosewood veneer is missing key plate and top plate, along with interior writing flaps, 9" x 12" x 4", c. 1860, $80.

Lap desk of rare tiger-stripe maple. Mother-of-pearl ornament on lid that may have been added later. Interior fittings are gone, 12-1/2" x 10" x 4", c. 1850, $75.

An odd size and shape characterize this man's walnut lap desk.
Brass key plate and brass plate in lid are missing, 8" x 10-1/2" x 5-
1/2", c. 1860, $90.

Desk in open position, odd flaps, no borders, no cover.

Lap desk of paper over pine resembles inlay, with tin key plate, purple velvet writing surface, rabbeted, c. 1890 $45.

Interior has elaborate paper border around writing flaps. An old pen was found in box.

Man's mahogany lap desk with satinwood stripes and inlay on lid and front is lined in original (real) gold foil paper. Very similar in style to document box pictured in previous chapter, 8" x 14" x 4-1/4", c. 1820, $175.

Walnut lap desk with black, painted banding on lid, 12" x 8" x 3-1/2" c. 1870, $75. *Private collection.*

Desk in open position.

Walnut, slant-lid lap desk with bronze stenciling and lock, 9" x 12" x 3", c. l970, $75.

Interior of desk with writing flap down to show gold leaf paper.

Letter Boxes

This seems to be the most logical label to attach to the many small boxes which do not seem to fit into any other category. Bigger than trinket boxes but smaller than document boxes, they could have been used to store letters or handkerchiefs or any small miscellaneous items. Some are elaborately decorated, others are unadorned. Most have locks. Some are lined in fabric or paper. The average size is about seven by ten inches. Many of the late-nineteenth century boxes have a greeting card pasted to the inside of the lid. The boxes were probably given as gifts. The card could have been pasted into the box by the recipient or the giver. Either way, it seems to have been one of those charming, long forgotten Victorian customs.

Letter box with rosewood veneer, coin silver bands, lock, handle on top missing, 9-1/2" x 3-1/4" x 2-1/4", c. 1850, $25.

Letter box of rosewood veneer over yellow pine with coin silver band, lock, 6-1/4" x 9-1/4" x 3", c. 1850, $60.

Letter box with rosewood veneer and silver banding. Almost identical to previous example except for key escutcheon, 6-1/4" x 9-1/4" x 3", c. 1850, $65.

Letter box of rosewood veneer with satinwood stripes and floral inlay, lined with yellow moiré paper; original key, 7-3/4" x 10-1/2" x 4" c. 1860, $75.

Inlay work on top of box.

Letter box of exotic wood with brass and blue enamel inlay, ripple molding, lock, 7-1/2" x 10-3/4" x 4-1/4", c. 1845, $100.

Pine letter or document box with new paint, lock, and handles, c. 1870, $20.

Interior of box where new paint is obvious, smeared around inside edge of lid.

Letter box with rosewood veneer, brass and mother-of-pearl inlay work, and brass stringing. Needs extensive repairs, 8-1/2" x 13" x 4", c. 1850, $45.

Letter box with original red paint, lapped, iron hasp, no lock. Traces of old decorations remain on lid, 6-1/2" x 10" x 5", c. 1860, $120. *Courtesy collection of Darlene Lesicko.*

Interior of box. "Scribbling" on lid is financial recording.

Pine letter box with old dark finish, green stripes, lock, 5" x 12" x 5", c. 1860, $85.

Letter box with drawer, pine, old finish, original knob, chip carving around edge of lid, 8" x 12" x 7", c. 1870, $145. *Courtesy Dianne L. Burton.*

Open box showing divider on right.

Liquor Chests   (see Cellarettes)

A type of liquor box popular in the mid-nineteenth century was known as a tantalus. The bottles were locked into place, visible but unreachable. The boxes were made of exotic wood and were probably made in England. The bottles were generally blown or cut glass.

Liquor chest of camphor wood with ebony finish, brass inlay and stringing, and a lock, c. 1880, $125.

The bottles are missing in the chest, which appears to be mahogany but is actually unfinished camphor wood.

Miniatures

Many collectors are fascinated by and collect only miniature versions of furniture, dishes, boxes, and many other objects. Little girls, and older ones too, treasured miniature versions of boxes such as blanket chests and lap desks. Miniature blanket chests complete with lock and till are thought to have been made by young men for their sweethearts.

Slide-top box with old, dark finish, could have been used to store small items such as brads or screws. Machine dovetailed from pine in the late nineteenth century, 1" x 2" x 2-1/2", $7.

A miniature blanket chest with grain paint, nailed, with leather hinges, 6" x 12" x 7-3/4", c. 1850, $200.

Dome-top pine box, old red paint, incised with a pansy spray, lock, mortise and tenon, 3" x 4-1/4" x 3", c. 1850 (paint added about 1900), $50.

Pine blanket chest with original brown paint, dovetailed, with lock and ivory escutcheon. Made without nails, 4-1/4" x 8-1/2" x 4", c. 1840, $850. *Courtesy collection of Darlene Lesicko.*

Interior of chest showing the lidded till.

Miniature treenware container, pine, original finish, 1" tall, plus lid. $35. *Courtesy Diana M. Dudley, Yesterday's Market and Chicken Coop.*

Blanket chest, grain painted over pine, lapped, no lock, 6-1/4 x 12-1/4" x 7", c. l850, $325. *Courtesy collection of Darlene Lesicko.*

Interior of chest with till.

Miniature slide-top box, cherry, dovetailed, with original finish, 3" x 4" x 2-3/8", c. l850, $100. *Courtesy James Hunsley.*

There was never any paint or stain on this miniature, cherry utility box, dovetailed, 6-3/4 x 11-1/2 x 6-1/2 inches, c. l850, $100. *Courtesy James Hunsley.*

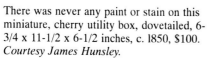

Pencil Boxes

Toward the end of the nineteenth century, when pencils began to take the place of slates in the classroom, the pencil box emerged as a necessary accessory for school. They were about eight inches long and opened out into three parts. There would be room for several pencils, erasers, and a small ruler. Most of them were painted or lithographed in bright primary colors. Plain undecorated lidded wooden boxes date from the early years of the twentieth century.

Dovetails are visible inside, along with applied molding around the lid.

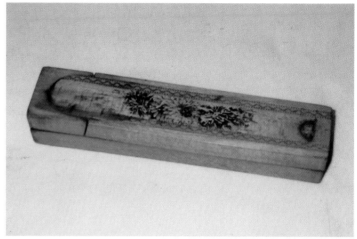

This floral decor pencil box was made with no hinges. The original owner scribbled his name on the bottom, along with the name of his school — Jersey County, Illinois, 2" x 9-1/4" x 1-5/8", c. 1900, $20.

When the lid comes off, there's a trough to keep pens and pencils in place. The bottom compartment was used for pen nibs, erasers, etc.

Pantry Boxes
(see Bentwood Boxes)

As the name indicates, these round, bentwood boxes were utilitarian storage boxes. Many of them were painted, more to preserve them than for decoration. Some of the later ones have a wire handle with a wood bail.

Pantry box with original green paint and wire handle indicates a late-nineteenth century manufacture, c. 1890, $250. *Courtesy collection of Darlene Lesicko.*

99

Pipe Boxes

Pyrography

Pipe boxes seem to have originated with the early Dutch (German) settlers in Pennsylvania and other eastern states. Pipe stems were long to accommodate long flowing beards. The boxes were long and rectangular and sometimes had a drawer in the bottom to hold spills or a tinder box. Most hung on the wall. They were made by local craftsmen out of available wood. Some are walnut or cherry, others soft woods that were painted or decorated. They are an easy item to copy or reproduce, so buyers should check carefully for signs of age such as scratches on the inside bottom and rusted square-cut nails.

Burnt wood or pyrography is the popular term for a craze of the late nineteenth century. This craft seems to have been practiced almost exclusively by women. A heated stylus was used to draw designs onto a soft wood such as pine. The heat from the stylus charred the wood just enough to leave a slight indentation. When a clear finish was applied, the design absorbed the shellac and turned black. There is nothing original about most pyrography. Patterns were sold in craft stores and catalogs. Some of the boxes or other articles came pre-stamped — a sort of paint-by-number concept. As always, a few individuals eschewed the pre-printed designs and made their own. These are the most sought after and the most difficult to find.

Generally most of these boxes have lost some of their original orange shellac finish. Orange shellac is not the easiest to obtain, but should be used if one wishes to restore the item to its nearly original finish.

Original paint marks this pine pipe box, made unusual by its two drawers; lapped, 9" x 19-1/2" x 5", $650. *Courtesy collection of Darlene Lesicko.*

A handkerchief or trinket box of pine with original finish, 8" x 8" x 3", c. 1900, $10.

The most commonly found pyrography box, probably a pre-designed kit, 4" x 12" x 3", c. 1900, $10.

Salt Boxes

From ancient times to the present, salt has been used to preserve and enhance the flavor of food. Until about 1870, when a process was invented to pulverize salt, it was lumpy and prone to clumping as it absorbed moisture. Salt that would be used within a short time was kept in a lidded box that generally hung on the wall near the stove or fireplace. The heat from the fire helped to keep the salt dry and usable. The boxes were simply made, generally nailed together, with a hinged, slanted lid. Wood was preferred since salt corrodes metal. Most are rectangular or square in shape. A late-nineteenth century style of salt box is the round, factory made type.

Made by an Amish craftsmen in Illinois, this hanging salt box has its original knob on the drawer and old red paint on nailed pine, 14-1/2" x 7-1/2" x 6-1/2", c. 1870, $300. *Courtesy collection of Darlene Lesicko.*

A round, hanging salt box of maple with brass label and hinged lid, c. 1890, $70.

Hanging salt box, pine old finish, nailed, 5" x 4-1/2" x 9", c. 1900 (factory made), $65.

Scouring Boxes

In the days when all food was prepared at home, a scouring box was needed to sharpen kitchen knives. The tray of the box was kept filled with pumice or fine sand and the knife was dipped into it and then honed on the attached hardwood slab. The knife blades could be stored in the sand or pumice to prevent rusting.

Pine scouring box, nailed, 15" x 10-1/2" x 3-1/2", $60. *Courtesy collection of Darlene Lesicko.*

Poplar scouring box, nailed, 19-1/2" x 11-1/2" x 3-1/2", late-nineteenth century, $60. *Private collection.*

Sewing Boxes

Before the sewing machine came into general use (about 1860) every little girl was taught to use the needle. Needlework samplers, highly prized today, were merely proof that the maker had mastered the art of stitching. Needlework was part of the curriculum of both public and private schools. Every item of clothing and every other item made of cloth was stitched together by hand, a time-consuming, never-ending process. The accouterments such as thread, scissors, and thimbles had to be kept together, and the sewing box was seldom out of use. Women of means had elaborate fitted boxes. Others had simpler but no less useful boxes.

A popular collectible today is the thread box. This simple, square box generally had a drawer and a compartment to hold thread. Most had a pin cushion on top. There were little port holes in the sides. Thread was strung through these holes. The thread was kept clean and the needed colors were readily visible. Some of these little boxes had a hidden mirror which could slide out and tilt to catch the light. Another accessory was the thimble box. Among the most desired boxes today are the simple boxes made by the Shakers, both for their own use and for the "worldly folk." The Midwestern Amish also made a distinct style of sewing box. Hardest to find are the large, elaborate fitted boxes, many of which were brought to the United States from China, both as gifts and as commercially salable items.

Sewing (spool) box of mahogany with satinwood stringing features ivory thread hole surrounds, and original pin cushion. A hidden mirror is stored over the drawer, c. 1850, $125.

Box with mirror out; ivory finials hold lid in place.

103

Mahogany with satinwood stringing sewing box includes ivory thread hole surrounds and hidden, framed mirror over drawer. Padding for the pincushion has been lost, c. 1830, $110.

Pine sewing box has original red paint, ivory thread hole surrounds, c. 1850, $130.

Open box reveals iron prongs for positioning spools. There should be one prong for each of the three "portholes."

Box with mirror in position to catch the light, could be adjusted by opening or closing the drawer.

Walnut sewing box has brass thread surrounds and revolves on its pedestal, c. 1850, $150.

Open box — center might once had held a pin cushion, or could have been for loose pins, buttons, etc.

Sewing box of cherry and maple. Wires that held the spools are gone, c. 1845, $85.

Chip-carved maple thread box has ivory porthole surrounds and ivory knob on lid, 6" x 6", c. 1840, $150.

Inside, a carved thimble holder sits in the center surrounded by wooden spool supports.

Possibly a sewing box, this rosewood veneered box has mother-of-pearl inlay, coin silver striping, bun feet, and wooden loop handles, 9" x 12" x 6-1/2", c. 1840, $180.

Inside are six covered compartments and a pin cushion. The tray, lined with the same silk as the compartment and the lid, lifts out.

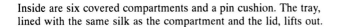

This sewing box sits on a revolving bird-cage stand and is made of rosewood with ivory banding and ivory escutcheon. The "ears" on the sides were for lamps or candles, c. 1830, $600.

One of two secret drawers pops out on a hidden spring mechanism when the center piece (second from right) is raised.

Inside are four covered compartments, the original pin cushion, original thread winders, a tray for pens, and a lift-out front tray that reveals a storage compartment beneath. The top once had a writing flap.

Amish sewing box is a plain, walnut construction with a drawer on the side and dome top, lapped, 5-1/2" x 10-3/4" x 5-1/4", c. 1860, $475. *Courtesy collection of Darlene Lesicko.*

Inside a pincushion is attached to the lid. The history of the box was handwritten by the granddaughter of the original owner.

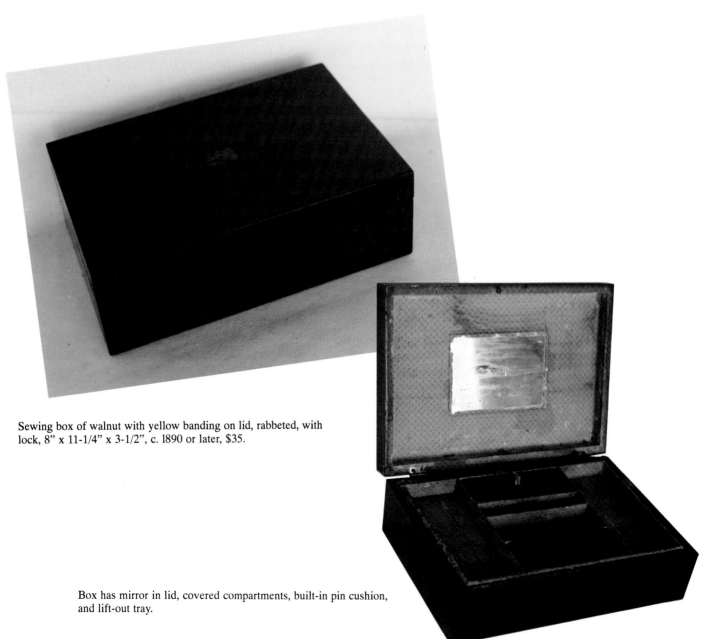

Sewing box of walnut with yellow banding on lid, rabbeted, with lock, 8" x 11-1/4" x 3-1/2", c. 1890 or later, $35.

Box has mirror in lid, covered compartments, built-in pin cushion, and lift-out tray.

Small thread box of cherry and maple holds one spool and includes ivory surround porthole, 3" x 3-1/4", c. 1860, $65.

Shipping Boxes

Late shipping boxes such as orange crates are prized for their labels. The boxes themselves are flimsy and of little interest. Early shipping boxes were often painted or paper covered. Some were built to withstand rough handling, moisture, and other perils. The labels or printed information reveal much about interests and habits in the nineteenth century.

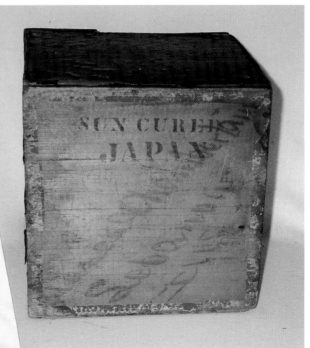

Bottom of the tea box.

Tea shipping box, nailed, with black paper covering, labeled "David O. Evans and Co. Importers of Teas." On the bottom, "Sun Cured Japan" is stamped and, faintly visible is written the name of a store in Lebanon, Illinois, 10" x 10" x 10", c. 1850, $25.

109

Snuff Boxes

Snuff is powdered tobacco. In the eighteenth and early nineteenth century, men and women of the aristocracy and upper classes inhaled snuff as part of a social ritual. The snuff was kept in a small box, which was taken out at an opportune moment and displayed as a status symbol. Many of these tiny, hinged boxes were made of precious metals (gold if one could afford it). A few were made of wood. These were often made as "whimsies." They could be shaped like animals, shoes, fruit, or vegetables. Snuff chewing was practiced by middle and working class people — often to dull the pain associated with bad teeth. Simple wooden boxes sometimes made with sliding lids were used as containers. Some are in the realm of folk art because of their unique decoration or carving.

A face is carved in the lid of this rare and possibly unique snuff box with old finish, 2-1/2" x 1-3/4", c. 1850, $150. *Private collection.*

Birch snuff box has old finish and Masonic symbols carved in lid, 3" x 1-1/2", c. 1850, $60. *Private collection.*

Box lip forms tight-fit for lid.

Soap Boxes

Soap boxes are similar to salt boxes in that they were a utilitarian object. A soap box does not have a lid and there is generally a drain hole in the base. They were hung near a wash stand or over a dry sink. Most are made of soft wood such as pine and were sometimes painted but not decorated. They are difficult to date as they were such a common household item. When they rotted out or broke it was a simple matter to make another one. They are always nailed together, not dovetailed.

Pine soap box with, blue paint and drain hole in base; nailed, 5" x 6" x 3-3/4", c. 1880, $40.

Spice Boxes

From antiquity, spices have been prized and highly coveted. Wars were fought over them and explorers were motivated by the possibility of riches beyond belief if they could only find a shorter trade route or a new source. In the days before refrigeration, spices were a necessity both to preserve and to disguise the taste of food which was going bad. Some spices such as bay could be grown in temperate climates, but most grew only in hot tropic climates. Like sugar and tea, spices were kept in locked containers. Also, each kind of spice was kept in a separate container.

The Pennsylvania Dutch spice cabinet is the most desired and most difficult to find. These spice boxes look like miniature cupboards with a locked door and little doors or boxes inside. They were highly prized by their original owners and were an indication of the wealth and status of the family. Common folk used a round bentwood box with little round lidded containers inside. A late, collectible spice box is the hanging type with eight drawers. These were made from about 1890 to 1920. Many were factory made and can be found in Sears and other catalogs of the time. They were simply constructed using nails. All kinds of spice boxes have been reproduced — even the late, eight-drawer type. The old boxes were used and the aroma of spices still lingers. Many of these hanging spice boxes are one of a kind, simply constructed by the man of the house. Paint and decoration, if any, were probably added by the housewife.

This spice box has five drawers, the largest being lined with copper and reserved for stick cinnamon. Probably painted originally, it has been refinished but still has the original knobs, 8-1/4" x 12", c. 1880, $200.

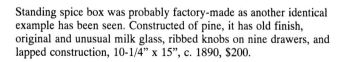

Pine spice box, refinished, was factory made and is easily found, 17" x 11" x 4", c. 1900, $190.

Standing spice box was probably factory-made as another identical example has been seen. Constructed of pine, it has old finish, original and unusual milk glass, ribbed knobs on nine drawers, and lapped construction, 10-1/4" x 15", c. 1890, $200.

Pine spice box with original finish is made highly desirable by its artfully detailed back piece, 11" x 9" x 3", c. 1880, $350. *Private collection.*

This type of spice box is avidly sought and seldom found. It has eleven drawers, original black, red, and salmon paint on pine and original knobs, 12" x 24" x 6", c. 1880, $950. *Courtesy collection of Darlene Lesicko.*

Original stenciled decor can be seen on the top drawer, and original graining is visible on back piece and bottom right drawer.

Another factory-made spice box with original or early paint and one hole for hanging, c. l900, $250. Courtesy Darlene Lesicko.

Spice box of pine with original grained paint and hand lettering. 9-1/4" x 13-3/4" x 4", c. 1890, $300. *Courtesy collection of Darlene Lesicko.*

Original, dark green paint covers pine spice box, 8-1/2" x 12" x 4-1/4", $300. *Courtesy collection of Darlene Lesicko.*

Factory made spice box of pine, 13-1/2" x 8-3/4" x 4-1/4" , c. 1900, $200. *Courtesy collection of Darlene Lesicko.*

Pine spice box with old, but not original, gray paint. This is among the most wanted of factory made boxes because its backboard is intact. Most boxes had the bottom two inches cut off so that the cabinet could stand on a shelf or counter, 18" x 11" x 5", c. 1900, $250. *Courtesy collection of Darlene Lesicko.*

Pine spice box with, old finish, original knobs, and square nail construction, 12" x 24" x 4", 1870 or earlier, $175. *Courtesy collection of Darlene Lesicko.*

Almost identical to the previous example, this one also has its original backboard along with several coats of paint, 18" x 11" x 5", c. 1900, $250. *Courtesy collection of Darlene Lesicko.*

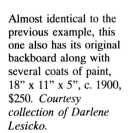

115

Drawers tilt on this unique spice box. Nails on the side are old if not original, and were used for hanging receipts, etc. The pine box was built using rabbeted construction, 13" x 21" x 6", c. 1870. The only way to set a price for a piece such as this is to place it in a well-established auction house and let the market determine the value. *Courtesy collection of Darlene Lesicko.*

Tilting drawers show original finish and knobs.

Stamp Boxes

Soon after stamps came into general use in England about 1840, someone devised a way to keep them dry and sorted by denomination. Stamps came into general use in the United States about 1845. These little compartmented boxes are often unrecognized for what they are. Some dealers call them ring or jewelry boxes.

A stamp box of soft wood, stained dark, with original finish, 2-1/2" x 4" x 1", c. 1850, $85. *Private collection.*

The decor and paint are not old on this dome-top stamp box made of pine, 6" x 2-3/4" x 2-3/4", c. 1850, $40.

Opened, the box reaveals three compartments with slanted sides to facilitate removal of stamps.

Inside the box are three compartments, also with new paint, made obvious by paint on the hinges — never seen on an original finish.

Sugar Buckets (Firkins)

A sugar bucket is a round container with a snug-fitting lid. They were used for storing dry staples. They would have been used for sugar, flour, rice, etc. Early ones have a wooden loop for a handle, later ones have a wire handle with a wooden hand grip. The wire-handled types are factory made, and sometimes were painted at the factory, sometimes by the original owner. Firken is another name for bucket.

A late sugar bucket, factory made, with old red paint, "finger" lapping, $275. *Courtesy collection of Darlene Lesicko.*

A pine sugar bucket, with lapped "fingers" and old blue paint, 12-1/2" x 8", $300. *Courtesy collection of Darlene Lesicko.*

"Sugar" is stamped on the lid of this early, pine bucket with traces of old paint, 9-3/4" x 9-3/4". *Courtesy collection of Darlene Lesicko.*

Sugar bucket with double "fingers" old finish, 12" tall, $550. *Courtesy collection of Darlene Lesicko.*

Wire handles on sugar buckets with original finish. Buckets originated in Alton, Illinois. Larger bucket, $225; smaller bucket, $175. *Courtesy collection of Darlene Lesicko.*

119

Sugar Chests

Sugar was once almost as scarce and luxurious as spices. Most people, if they used sweetening at all, relied on honey. Sugar was not the granulated and refined product we know today. It was brownish in color, and hard. It had to be clipped or chopped before it could be used. In the days when household necessities were purchased by the box or barrel rather than in pounds or ounces, it was necessary to have adequate storage facilities. The sugar chest served such a purpose. Sugar chests looked a little bit like blanket chests except that they stood on legs and had compartments for sugar and other luxuries such as tea or coffee. There was always a lock. These chests are generally found only in the South, according to furniture historians. A chest similar in style but more crudely made is being brought into the United States from Mexico. They may have some age, but they are not sugar chests. The American chests are hardwood and are of dovetailed construction. A similar but smaller version of the sugar chest is the tabletop box, which generally held about twenty pounds of sugar.

Open box shows details of construction.

Sugar box with old red paint over cherry, dovetailed, has a drawer for utensils or spices. The drawer and the box both have locks, 15" x 9" x 9", c. 1870, $300. *Private collection.*

Tea Caddies

Tea, along with sugar, coffee, and spices, was a luxury before the American Revolution. The ritual of afternoon tea was an English custom brought here by the early colonists. The Dutch, Germans, and Irish also brought their tea-drinking customs with them from the "old country." The dried tea leaves were stored in a container called a caddy. Some of the more elaborate caddies had two inner boxes and a bowl (a mixer). All tea caddies are fitted with a lock.

Some boxes were lined in either tinfoil or leather (shagreen). Many were made in England and Ireland, but the simpler ones were probably made in the United States. Many of these boxes might have been made by an apprentice finishing his training — finding two alike is next to impossible. Mahogany, walnut, rosewood and other exotic woods were used to make tea caddies.

Sarcophagus-shaped tea caddy with exotic wood veneer, two silver-foil lined boxes with hinged lids, shagreen (leather) lining, bun feet of ivory, and brass handle on lid, probably made in England, 6-1/4" x 12-1/4" x 7", c. 1820, $200.

Lined with red leather, the caddy contains two inner boxes with satinwood banding. The mixing bowl is missing.

Tea caddy of tortoise shell over pine with two interior boxes, 9" x 4-3/4" x 9", c. 1820, $250.

Open lid reveals two inner boxes with slip-on lids, no hinges, lined with silver foil.

Inlay work with exotic wood and walnut graces this domed-top tea caddy, now missing its interior fittings, 6" x 8-1/2" x 5-1/2", c. 1830, $100.

Tea caddy, Chinese laquerware on pine, 6-1/8" x 4" x 3-1/2", c. 1840, $75.

Elaborate mother-of-pearl and coin silver work on solid rosewood could have been done by a sailor or anyone else who spent much time at sea, 5-1/4" x 8-5/8" x 5-1/8", c. 1840, $300.

Tea caddy is constructed of exotic burled wood with brass, enamel, and abalone shell inlay. The interior fittings are gone, 6-1/4" x 11-1/2" x 5-3/4", c. 1830, $250.

Interior partitions indicate that box once had two smaller boxes inside.

Tea caddy box from a larger box.

Tea caddy of walnut with satinwood stringing on lid, original brass handle, and small bun feet; dovetailed and made in the United States, 10" x 5-1/2" x 5", c. 1830, $100.

Tea caddy "whimsey" in pear shape made from walnut. The blush on the pear matches the blush on the lid when properly aligned. Whimsies were not used for storage of tea per se, but were used as part of the tea service. They held only enough tea for one meal. Some of them had locks and hinged lids, but this one never did, 5-1/2" x 8", c. 1820, $200.

Burled wood apple tea caddy whimsey is missing stem on lid, 4-1/4" tall, c. 1820, $80.

Tea caddy of satinwood with exotic wood inlay and ivory escutcheon is either English or Irish, 6-1/2" x 5" x 5", c. 1820, $150. *Private collection.*

There were never boxes inside. The lid shows an old repair to the handle.

Tool Boxes

Every artisan had and has a tool box. Tool boxes could be a book in themselves. There are watchmakers boxes, carpenters boxes, wheelwright boxes, stencilers boxes, tinkers (tin repairers) boxes, . . . the list could go on. Wallpaper hangers had long rectangular boxes to store and carry their folding table and ruler, which was often six feet long. The purpose of many of these boxes, when their contents are gone, is a mystery to present day collectors. Most of these boxes are "one of a kind," except for late tool boxes. The original owner made the box or had it made to his specifications and needs.

A stenciler's or china painter's box is fitted with compartments for bottles, brushes, and mixing bowls. It has black paint over pine and has a lithograph picture on the lid, 7-1/2" x 12" x 1-1/2", c. 1890, $25.

Open box, from page 125 bottom photo, with original bottles containing various powders and one milk glass mixing bowl.

Tool carrier of nailed pine with old, green paint is similar to a cutlery box but heavier. The box descended in the Burgess family and was always used for storing small tools, c. 1890, $40.

Toy Boxes

From the mid-nineteen hundreds until well into the twentieth century, blocks were a favored toy. The brightly colored lithographed squares could be arranged to make various pictures. Many of them were religious in nature, showing various stories from the Bible. They came in wooden boxes with a picture (in color) on the lid. Because of their religious themes, they were probably considered a suitable Sunday toy.

Painted pine box with twelve wooden blocks which could be arranged to form various classic scenes. This one is St. George and the Dragon. The cover shows three angels blessing a kneeling knight. One angel appears to be holding the holy grail, which only Sir Percival was allowed to see because his heart was pure. The puzzle is called Pilgrim's Progress, but the pictures are from tales of King Arthur, $100. *Courtesy Shirl's Dolls, Yesterdays Market.*

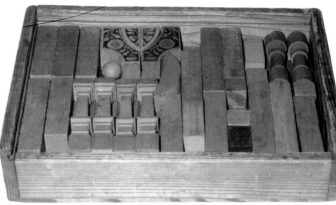

Pine box with pieces similar to Lincoln Logs, c. 1900, $60. *Courtesy Shirl's Dolls, Yesterday's Market.*

Pine box with lithographed scene on cover, slide top. Wooden pieces of different sizes could be used to create buildings, $60. *Courtesy Shirl's Dolls, Yesterday's Market.*

Pine box, top missing, contains twelve lithographed blocks, c. 1900, $50. *Courtesy Shirl's Dolls, Yesterday's Market.*

Pine box with sliding top and lithographed picture called Prize Animals, c. 1900, $250. *Courtesy collection of Darlene Lesicko.*

The blocks are clean and unfaded.

Tramp Art

Tramp Art is a type of chip carving practiced by whittlers and semiskilled wood carvers, probably from about 1870 through the Depression years. Shipping crates and other cheap softwoods were the mediums used. They are a form of American folk art since the creators were self-taught and made whatever they fancied. The best show originality in the use of form and often times color. The maker whittled out pieces of wood and then glued them together to form a design unlike chip carving in which a single layer of wood was utilized. All sorts of useful and fanciful things were made — dressing boxes, sewing boxes, hanging boxes, picture frames. The creator was limited only by his skill and the amount of material he had to work with.

A rare, tramp art spice box with original finish and knobs, made of nailed pine, 16" x 10" x 5", c. 1900-1910, $650. *Courtesy collection of Darlene Lesicko.*

Square box topped by brass knob. The lid was made of fourteen layers of wood glued together, 7" x 8" x 7", c. 1890, $250. *Courtesy Dianne L. Burton.*

The inside of the lid and bottom of the box illustrate the work that went into tramp art. The creators invariably started with a plain box, often a cigar or other thin wood box, and proceeded to embellish it. The lid was probably part of a tea box originally, and the base was part of a candy or cigar box.

The base is old, but the embellishment was done within the last five years. *Courtesy of Dianne L. Burton.*

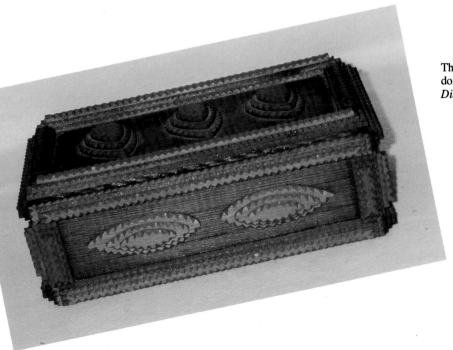

This sewing box and the next were made by J. Goetz and presented to Miss Knoppel in 1891 and 1890. it has lift-out tray and lock, original finish, 12" x 7" x 7". *Courtesy Dianne L. Burton.*

Inside is the original mirror.

The lid is formed from three layers of carved wood.

The mate to the preceding box, this one is hinged with a lock, velvet lined interior, and original finish, 5" x 8" x 4", $650 for pair. *Courtesy of Dianne L. Burton.*

Possibly used as a document box, pieces of this size and detail are rare. It's in almost perfect, original condition. Hinged with lock and original brass paw feet, 18" x 12" x 8", c. 1880, $500. *Courtesy Dianne L. Burton.*

Inside there was once a tray. Velvet lining and brass handles are intact.

Tramp art box with scalloped carving, pine, hinged, no lock, 7" x 9" x 8", c. 1900, $125. *Courtesy of Dianne L. Burton.*

Treenware

Treenware is a term for utilitarian wooden ware made for kitchen use. The items are made by hollowing out a block of wood rather than by joining. Most old treenware consists of items such as spice containers, mortar and pestle sets, round covered jars, etc. Treen was sometimes decorated but seldom painted except for Pease wear. The Pease family worked in Ohio in the mid-and late-eighteen hundreds.

This treenware box may have been used for snuff. The lid has a bone knob and chip carving, 3" x 2", $150. *Private collection.*

Box and lid.

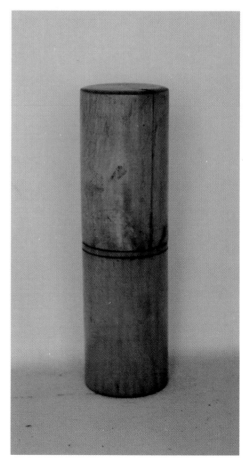

The original use for this tall, cylindrical treenware box is unknown, though it could have been used to hold harness maker's needles. Made of birch, c. 1900?, $15.

Treen bowl may have had lid originally; chip carving, old finish, c. 1870,
$10. *Courtesy of Yesterday's Market/
Judy McDonald*

Trinket Boxes

Trinket boxes include a wide variety of styles and
woods. Many were made of exotic woods in small factories
and cabinet making shops. Young men made them for their
sweethearts. Many resemble letter boxes except in size. For
definitive purposes, a trinket box should be no more than
about six or seven inches long. See chapter Letter Boxes.

Interior lined with an old letter.

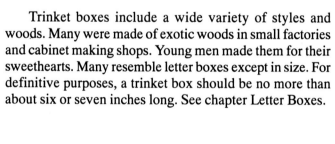

Trinket box of rosewood veneer with satinwood inlay, 4-1/2" x
6-1/2" x 2-1/2", c. 1850, $40.

Trinket box painted black over pine with gold scroll work and a bird painted on lid, lined with purple paper. The bottom is cardboard — often used on late-nineteenth century boxes of this type, 6-1/2" x 9-1/2" x 3", c. 1890, $15.

Trinket box painted black over pine with floral decor on lid, gold scroll work, and lock; cardboard bottom, 6-1/4" x 8-1/2" x 3", c. 1890, $15.

Trinket box of solid rosewood with lock, 7-1/2" x 6-1/2" x 3", c. 1850, $25.

Trinket box of rosewood with star inlay on lid; lock, 6" x 8" x 3", c. l860, $30.

Open box with old greeting card pasted in the lid advertising a spice company

Trinket box of walnut with hand-painted floral design on lid; no lock; inside painted blue, 3-3/8" x 6-3/4" x 2", c. 1850, $50.

A trinket box of exotic wood veneer with hand-painted floral design on lid, lined in original red silk, 4" x 4-1/2" x 2-1/2", lock, c. 1845, $50.

Trinket box of pine with burled wood and satinwood inlay, canted corners, and lock, 5-1/2" x 7-1/2" x 3-1/2", c. l860, $30.

Interior lined with German-language newspaper.

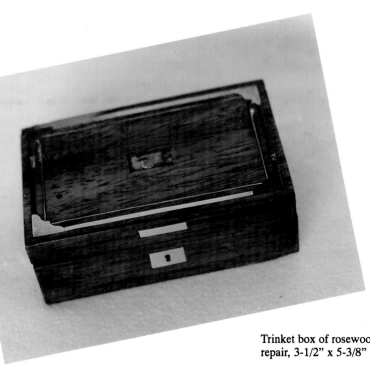

Trinket box of rosewood and coin silver inlay with lock, needs repair, 3-1/2" x 5-3/8" x 1-7/8", c. l840, $15 as is.

Trinket box with rosewood veneer, satinwood inlay, and lock, 4-1/2"
x 6-1/2" x 2", c. l860, $40.

Trinket box with solid, carved top,
mahogany veneered sides, and lock, 6" x 7"
x 2-3/4", c. l870, $35.

Lid of box with inlay around carving
missing.

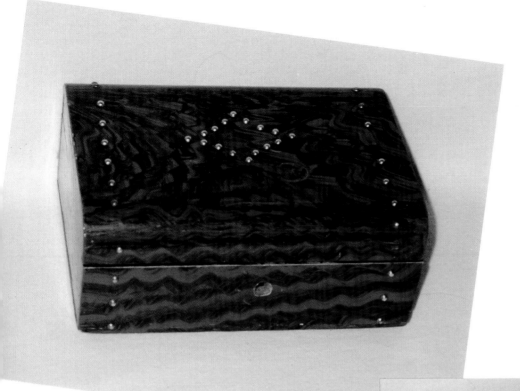

Trinket box with original red- and black-grain painting over pine; brass nail head studs, 6-3/4" x 4-3/4" x 2-3/4", $35.

Open box with greeting card pasted in lid.

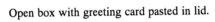

Trinket box painted to resemble rosewood, with brass bands, lock, and escutcheon inscribed "souvenir," 4" x 4" x 3", c. 1860, $25.

Wall Boxes

"Wall boxes" encompass a wide range of useful and fanciful objects from the simple salt box to the elaborately carved and decorated hanging paper rack popular in the later years of the nineteenth century. They served many useful purposes. Objects such as matches could be kept out of the reach of children. A soap box would be hung near the wash basin or sink. In the early years of the nineteenth century when clocks and watches were rare and expensive, a pocket watch would be hung in a little wall box so all could see the time.

Wall or standing box, green paint over oak, possibly used for candles. The back was cut out to form initials, c. 1870, $150.

Wall box of mahogany veneer with satinwood and ebony inlay, satinwood stringing. Possibly used for storing candles, c. 1800, $300.

Hanging box painted gray over walnut, possibly used for candles, c. 1860, $250. *Courtesy collection of Darlene Lesicko.*

A wall box with old yellow paint and decoration over nailed pine. Mid-nineteenth century, age of decoration uncertain, $90.

Walnut hanging box, nailed, hung in White Hall, Illinois, hotel, c. 1880, $30.

Spoon holder of walnut with old finish, $450. *Private collection.*

Walnut wall box, nailed, with old green paint and pinwheels incised into back and base, 4-1/2" x 7-3/4" x 2-1/8", $165. *Courtesy collection of Darlene Lesicko.*

Wall storage box, may have been used for spices. Pine, nailed, with original paint and knobs, 12" x 6-1/2" x 4-1/4", $100. *Courtesy collection of Darlene Lesicko.*

Pine wall box painted chromium yellow over red with serrated edging on backboard, 16" x 7-1/4" x 5", $300. *Courtesy collection of Darlene Lesicko.*

Possibly a comb box; nailed pine, $80. *Courtesy collection of Darlene Lesicko.*

Pine wall box with old, light green paint, nailed. Possibly used for soap, $150. *Courtesy collection of Darlene Lesicko.*

Wood (Kindling) Boxes

When wood burning stoves took the place of fireplaces, one major change was the size of the logs burned. Fireplaces required large logs as much of the heat went up the chimney. Cook stoves and heating stoves required small slabs of wood or chunks of coal. The stove needed frequent refueling. A large, lidded box was kept near the stove. One of the first chores assigned to country children was keeping the wood box filled.

The top shelf of this wood box held various kitchen items such as pans or buckets. Nailed pine with grain paint and hinged lid, 23" x 22", late-nineteenth century, $300. *Private collection.*

Writing Boxes

Writing boxes are often confused with lap desks. The two are similar, but not identical. The writing box held papers, pens, ink, etc., but had no flap or writing surface. Many of them are quite elaborate and have secret compartments. They also tend to be larger than lap desks. They are not nearly as common as lap desks.

Writing box of solid rosewood with brass stringing and inlay; inside fittings intact, 11-1/2" x 18-3/4" x 8", c. 1840, $350.

Lid held pamphlets, booklets, etc.

Fittings include five lids and a center tray that lifts out.

With the lids open, a secret compartment is revealed in the far left front.

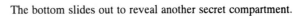

The bottom slides out to reveal another secret compartment.

Miscellaneous Boxes

In this category are all the big, and little, boxes that do not seem to fit anywhere else. Many painted boxes pose a puzzle. Which is paramount — the unique decoration or the original purpose of the box? A box might have been made to house a special object. Miniatures also are puzzling to categorize. Do they belong with their larger counterparts or should they be in a category of their own?

Mahogany desk box with painted decor and ink stand, two ink bottles, bail (handle), and drawer, English. c. 1870, $150.

Pine box with old red paint, leather hinges, and numbers painted on sides. Age and original use are a mystery, $10.

Storage box made of pine with old finish and gold striping and stenciling, brass feet, no lock. Was being used as a sewing box when found, though that probably wasn't its original use. The box presents a dilemma: the top is badly worn, but if refinished the original stenciling will be lost, c. 1870, $50.

Storage box of old red finish on pine, dome top, dovetail construction; no lock, 14" x 8" x 8", c. 1850, $200. *Courtesy of Rees Antiques on the Square, Carlinville, Illinois.*

Open box reveals dovetailed front, nailed back. It may have been cut down from a larger size box.

Possibly used by the military, this pine trunk has an old, dark finish, c. 1830?, $85.

The trunk was lined with newspapers from the 1830s.

Stacked storage boxes have their original paint, c. 1860s, $250 each. *Courtesy collection of Darlene Lesicko.*

A box used by beekeepers to move the queen has old blue paint, handholds on the sides, and a lift top, nailed, c. 1900, $200. *Courtesy collection of Darlene Lesicko.*

Beekeeper's box has a removable glass panel on the side, fixed glass above.

Possibly used as a bottle rack, this box has its old finish, wire dividers, and square nails, c. 1880, $15.

Pine cupboard has old paint. It is not a box, but it's too interesting not to show. Original use unknown, c. 1880, $400. *Courtesy collection of Darlene Lesicko.*

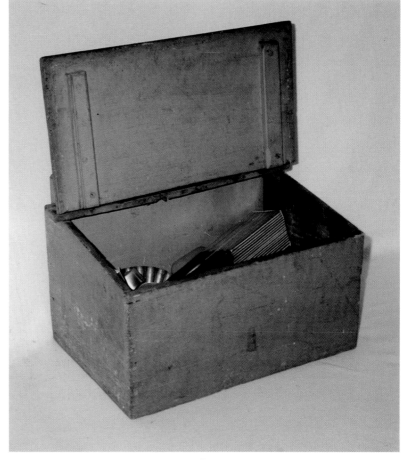

Painted gray pine storage box has no lock. Original use unknown, c. 1880, $150. *Courtesy collection of Darlene Lesicko.*

Diplomat's box may have been used for calling cards. Made of solid rosewood with solid silver mountings, 10" x 6-1/4" x 3", $120.

The top of the box has a center medallion empressed "Estados Unidos de Brazil 15 de November de 1889."

Interior lined in rose-colored silk.

Possibly a Victorian novelty thimble holder, this box is made of walnut with applied moldings shaped like acorns and a turned lid, c. 1870, $75.

A box cut from one piece of wood in the mid-eighteenth century was made to hold a Catholic missal (prayer book) dated 1778. It was brought to America by ancestors of present owner. *Private collection.*

Oak box, dovetailed, with old finish, c. 1760, $80. *Private collection.*

Inside, a small divider on the right does not reveal its purpose.

A storage box with old red paint, cleats on sides of lid, no lock, c. 1850, $80. *Private collection.*

This box is old, the decoration contemporary; dated 1981 on base with artist's initials, $45. *Courtesy of Yesterday's Market/Mark Miller.*

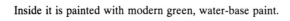

Inside it is painted with modern green, water-base paint.

Homemade box used to store a concertina is interesting because of the oak graining, popular in the late-nineteenth century, and also used on furniture and woodwork. $40. *Courtesy collection of Darlene Lesicko.*

Stringholder on pedestal. The bowl is made from one piece of walnut, with a notch cut in the side to facilitate removal of string. Used in stores, 11" x 7", c. 1900, $150.

Stringholder with lid removed.

Fretwork design was cut with a jigsaw from wood such as mahogany or cedar. Few examples of such work remain because it is easily broken. The lid has a design of a dove and the words "remember me," 6" x 12" x 3", c. 1900, $40.

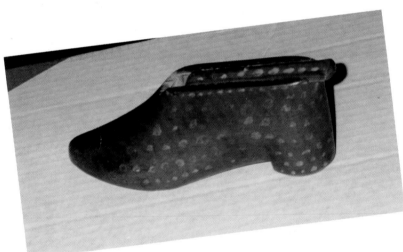

"Trick" box is paint decorated with a sliding top, 5" long, c. 1850, $200. *Courtesy collection of Darlene Lesicko.* 432.

When lid is opened a snake pops out.

Commercial storage box for coffee beans made of painted pine, 30" x 24", circa 1880, $300. *Courtesy collection of Darlene Lesicko.*

Ink bottle holder is carved and incised, with original paint, 3" tall, c. 1890, $25. *Courtesy of Yesterday's Market/Judy McDonald.*

Pine trinket box is covered in velvet and needlepoint. This would have been considered a proper gift for a young woman to give to a man, 4" x 7", c. 1870, $20.

The box comes apart and the lid has sprinkling holes.

Stetson box held powder used to facilitate removal of leather gloves, c. 1900, $30.

Scent holder with exotic wood and gold mountings, 1-1/4". *Courtesy of Diane Dudley.*

Crossbow bolt quiver, purchased in Bosnia, with chip carving, c. 1800 or earlier. *Courtesy of Yesterday's Market/Diane Dudley.*